Exotics and Retrospectives

EXOTICS AND
RETROSPECTIVES

By LAFCADIO HEARN
LECTURER ON ENGLISH LITERATURE
IN THE IMPERIAL UNIVERSITY, TŌKYŌ

AUTHOR OF "OUT OF THE EAST,"
"GLIMPSES OF UNFAMILIAR JAPAN," &c.

BOSTON
LITTLE, BROWN, AND COMPANY
1923

Copyright, 1898

By Little, Brown, and Co.

———

ALL but one of the papers composing this volume appear for the first time. The little essays, or rather fantasies, forming the second part of the book, deal with experiences in two hemispheres; but their general title should explain why they have been arranged independently of that fact. To any really scientific imagination, the curious analogy existing between certain teachings of evolutional psychology and certain teachings of Eastern faith, — particularly the Buddhist doctrine that all sense-life is Karma, and all substance only the phenomenal result of acts and thoughts, — might have suggested something much more significant than my cluster of *Retrospectives*. These are offered merely as intimations of a truth incomparably less difficult to recognize than to define.

L. H.

TŌKYŌ, JAPAN,
February 15, 1898.

Contents

List of Illustrations

Full Page

Illustrations in the Text

Exotics

— "Even the worst tea is sweet when first made from the new leaf." — *Japanese proverb.*

Exotics and Retrospectives

Fuji-no-Yama

Kité miréba,
Sahodo madé nashi,
Fuji no Yama !

Seen on close approach, the mountain of Fuji does not
come up to expectation. — *Japanese proverbial philosophy.*

T HE most beautiful sight in Japan, and certainly one of the most beautiful in the
world, is the distant apparition of Fuji on
cloudless days, — more especially days of spring
and autumn, when the greater part of the peak
is covered with late or with early snows. You
can seldom distinguish the snowless base, which
remains the same color as the sky : you perceive
only the white cone seeming to hang in heaven ;
and the Japanese comparison of its shape to an
inverted half-open fan is made wonderfully exact
by the fine streaks that spread downward from
the notched top, like shadows of fan-ribs. Even

lighter than a fan the vision appears, — rather
the ghost or dream of a fan; — yet the material
reality a hundred miles away is grandiose among
the mountains of the globe. Rising to a height
of nearly 12,500 feet, Fuji is visible from thirteen
provinces of the Empire. Nevertheless it is one
of the easiest of lofty mountains to climb; and
for a thousand years it has been scaled every
summer by multitudes of pilgrims. For it is
not only a sacred mountain, but the most sacred
mountain of Japan, — the holiest eminence of
the land that is called Divine, — the Supreme
Altar of the Sun; — and to ascend it at least once
in a life-time is the duty of all who reverence
the ancient gods. So from every district of the
Empire pilgrims annually wend their way to
Fuji; and in nearly all the provinces there are
pilgrim-societies — *Fuji-Kō,* — organized for the
purpose of aiding those desiring to visit the
sacred peak. If this act of faith cannot be performed by everybody in person, it can at least
be performed by proxy. Any hamlet, however
remote, can occasionally send one representative
to pray before the shrine of the divinity of Fuji,
and to salute the rising sun from that sublime
eminence. Thus a single company of Fuji-

pilgrims may be composed of men from a hundred different settlements.

By both of the national religions Fuji is held in reverence. The Shintō deity of Fuji is the beautiful goddess Ko-no-hana-saku-ya-himé, — she who brought forth her children in fire without pain, and whose name signifies " Radiant-blooming-as-the-flowers-of-the-trees," or, according to some commentators, " Causing-the-flowers-to-blossom-brightly." On the summit is her temple ; and in ancient books it is recorded that mortal eyes have beheld her hovering, like a luminous cloud, above the verge of the crater. Her viewless servants watch and wait by the precipices to hurl down whomsoever presumes to approach her shrine with unpurified heart. . . . Buddhism loves the grand peak because its form is like the white bud of the Sacred Flower, — and because the eight cusps of its top, like the eight petals of the Lotos, symbolize the Eight Intelligences of Perception, Purpose, Speech, Conduct, Living, Effort, Mindfulness, and Contemplation.

But the legends and traditions about Fuji, the stories of its rising out of the earth in a single night, — of the shower of pierced-jewels once flung down from it, — of the first temple built upon its summit eleven hundred years ago, — of the Luminous Maiden that lured to the crater an Emperor who was never seen afterward, but is still worshipped at a little shrine erected on the place of his vanishing, — of the sand that daily rolled down by pilgrim feet nightly reascends to its former position, — have not all these things been written in books? There is really very little left for me to tell about Fuji except my own experience of climbing it.

I made the ascent by way of Gotemba, — the least picturesque, but perhaps also the least difficult of the six or seven routes open to choice. Gotemba is a little village chiefly consisting of pilgrim-inns. You reach it from Tōkyō in about three hours by the Tōkaidō railway, which rises for miles as it approaches the neighborhood of the mighty volcano. Gotemba is considerably more than two thousand feet above the sea, and therefore comparatively cool in the hottest season. The open country about it slopes to Fuji; but the slope is so gradual that the table-land seems almost level to the eye. From Gotemba in perfectly clear weather the mountain looks uncomfortably near, — formidable by proximity, —

though actually miles away. During the rainy
season it may appear and disappear alternately
many times in one day, — like an enormous
spectre. But on the grey August morning when
I entered Gotemba as a pilgrim, the landscape
was muffled in vapors; and Fuji was totally
invisible. I arrived too late to attempt the ascent
on the same day; but I made my preparations at
once for the day following, and engaged a couple
of *gōriki* (" strong-pull men "), or experienced
guides. I felt quite secure on seeing their broad
honest faces and sturdy bearing. They supplied
me with a pilgrim-staff, heavy blue *tabi* (that is
to say, cleft-stockings, to be used with sandals), a
straw hat shaped like Fuji, and the rest of a
pilgrim's outfit; — telling me to be ready to
start with them at four o'clock in the morning.

What is hereafter set down consists of notes
taken on the journey, but afterwards amended
and expanded, — for notes made while climbing
are necessarily hurried and imperfect.

1

August 24th, 1897.

From strings stretched above the balcony upon which my inn-room opens, hundreds of towels are hung like flags, — blue towels and white, having printed upon them in Chinese characters the names of pilgrim-companies and of the divinity of Fuji. These are gifts to the house, and serve as advertisements. . . . Raining from a uniformly grey sky. Fuji always invisible.

August 25th.

3 : 30 *a. m.* — No sleep ; — tumult all night of parties returning late from the mountain, or arriving for the pilgrimage ; — constant clapping of hands to summon servants ; — banqueting and singing in the adjoining chambers, with alarming bursts of laughter every few minutes. . . . Breakfast of soup, fish, and rice. Gōriki arrive in professional costume, and find me ready. Nevertheless they insist that I shall undress again and put on heavy underclothing ; — warning me that even when it is Doyō (the period of greatest summer heat) at the foot of the mountain, it is

Daikan (the period of greatest winter cold) at the top. Then they start in advance, carrying provisions and bundles of heavy clothing. . . . A kuruma waits for me, with three runners, — two to pull, and one to push, as the work will be hard uphill. By kuruma I can go to the height of five thousand feet.

Morning black and slightly chill, with fine rain ; but I shall soon be above the rain-clouds. . . . The lights of the town vanish behind us ; —the kuruma is rolling along a country-road. Outside of the swinging penumbra made by the paper-lantern of the foremost runner, nothing is clearly visible ; but I can vaguely distinguish silhouettes of trees and, from time to time, of houses, — peasants' houses with steep roofs.

Grey wan light slowly suffuses the moist air ; — day is dawning through drizzle. . . . Gradually the landscape defines with its colors. The way lies through thin woods. Occasionally we pass houses with high thatched roofs that look like farmhouses ; but cultivated land is nowhere visible. . . .

Open country with scattered clumps of trees, — larch and pine. Nothing in the horizon but

scraggy tree-tops above what seems to be the rim
of a vast down.   No sign whatever of Fuji. . . .
For the first time I notice that the road is black,
— black sand and cinders apparently, volcanic
cinders : the wheels of the kuruma and the feet
of the runners sink into it with a crunching
sound.

The rain has stopped, and the sky becomes
a clearer grey. . . . The trees decrease in size
and number as we advance.

What I have been taking for the horizon, in
front of us, suddenly breaks open, and begins to
roll smokily away to left and right.   In the great
rift part of a dark-blue mass appears, — a portion
of Fuji.   Almost at the same moment the sun
pierces the clouds behind us ; but the road now
enters a copse covering the base of a low ridge,
and the view is cut off. . . . Halt at a little
house among the trees, — a pilgrims' resting-
place, — and there find the gōriki, who have
advanced much more rapidly than my runners,
waiting for us.   Buy eggs, which a gōriki rolls
up in a narrow strip of straw matting ; — tying
the matting tightly with straw cord between the
eggs, — so that the string of eggs has somewhat

the appearance of a string of sausages. . . .
Hire a horse.

Sky clears as we proceed; — white sunlight
floods everything. Road reascends; and we
emerge again on the moorland. And, right in
front, Fuji appears, — naked to the summit, —
stupendous, — startling as if newly risen from
the earth. Nothing could be more beautiful.
A vast blue cone, — warm-blue, almost violet
through the vapors not yet lifted by the sun,
— with two white streaklets near the top which
are great gullies full of snow, though they look
from here scarcely an inch long. But the charm
of the apparition is much less the charm of color
than of symmetry, — a symmetry of beautiful
bending lines with a curve like the curve of a
cable stretched over a space too wide to allow of
pulling taut. (This comparison did not at once
suggest itself : The first impression given me by
the grace of those lines was an impression of
femininity ; — I found myself thinking of some
exquisite sloping of shoulders towards the neck.)
I can imagine nothing more difficult to draw at
sight. But the Japanese artist, through his marvellous skill with the writing-brush, — the skill

inherited from generations of calligraphists, —
easily faces the riddle : he outlines the silhouette
with two flowing strokes made in the fraction of
a second, and manages to hit the exact truth of
the curves, — much as a professional archer might
hit a mark, without consciously taking aim,
through long exact habit of hand and eye.

II

I see the gōriki hurrying forward far away, —
one of them carrying the eggs round his neck!
. . . Now there are no more trees worthy of the
name, — only scattered stunted growths resembling shrubs. The black road curves across a vast
grassy down; and here and there I see large black
patches in the green surface, — bare spaces of ashes
and scoriæ; showing that this thin green skin
covers some enormous volcanic deposit of recent
date. . . . As a matter of history, all this district
was buried two yards deep in 1707 by an eruption
from the side of Fuji. Even in far-off Tōkyō
the rain of ashes covered roofs to a depth of six-
teen centimetres. There are no farms in this
region, because there is little true soil; and there

is no water. But volcanic destruction is not eternal destruction; eruptions at last prove fertilizing; and the divine " Princess-who-causes-the-flowers-to-blossom-brightly " will make this waste to smile again in future hundreds of years.

. . . The black openings in the green surface become more numerous and larger. A few dwarf-shrubs still mingle with the coarse grass. . . . The vapors are lifting; and Fuji is changing color. It is no longer a glowing blue, but a dead sombre blue. Irregularities previously hidden by rising ground appear in the lower part of the grand curves. One of these to the left, — shaped like a camel's hump, — represents the focus of the last great eruption.

The land is not now green with black patches, but black with green patches; and the green patches dwindle visibly in the direction of the peak. The shrubby growths have disappeared. The wheels of the kuruma, and the feet of the runners sink deeper into the volcanic sand. . . . The horse is now attached to the kuruma with ropes, and I am able to advance more rapidly. Still the mountain seems far away; but we are really running up its flank at a height of more than five thousand feet.

Fuji has ceased to be blue of any shade. It is
black, — charcoal-black, — a frightful extinct heap
of visible ashes and cinders and slaggy lava. . . .
Most of the green has disappeared. Likewise all
of the illusion. The tremendous naked black
reality, — always becoming more sharply, more
grimly, more atrociously defined, — is a stupefaction, a nightmare. . . . Above — miles above —
the snow patches glare and gleam against that
blackness, — hideously. I think of a gleam of
white teeth I once saw in a skull, — a woman's
skull, — otherwise burnt to a sooty crisp.

So one of the fairest, if not the fairest of earthly
visions, resolves itself into a spectacle of horror
and death. . . . But have not all human ideals
of beauty, like the beauty of Fuji seen from afar,
been created by forces of death and pain ? — are
not all, in their kind, but composites of death,
beheld in retrospective through the magical haze
of inherited memory ?

III

The green has utterly vanished ; — all is black.
There is no road, — only the broad waste of
black sand sloping and narrowing up to those
dazzling, grinning patches of snow. But there
is a track, — a yellowish track made by thousands and thousands of cast-off sandals of straw
(*waraji*), flung aside by pilgrims. Straw sandals
quickly wear out upon this black grit ; and every
pilgrim carries several pair for the journey. Had
I to make the ascent alone, I could find the path
by following that wake of broken sandals, — a
yellow streak zigzagging up out of sight across
the blackness.

6 : 40 *a. m.* — We reach Tarōbō, first of the
ten stations on the ascent : height, 6000 feet.
The station is a large wooden house, of which
two rooms have been fitted up as a shop for the
sale of staves, hats, raincoats, sandals, — everything pilgrims need. I find there a peripatetic
photographer offering for sale photographs of
the mountain which are really very good as
well as very cheap. . . . Here the gōriki take

their first meal; and I rest. The kuruma can
go no further; and I dismiss my three runners,
but keep the horse, — a docile and surefooted
creature; for I can venture to ride him up to
Ni-gō-goséki, or Station No. 2½.

Start for No. 2½ up the slant of black sand,
keeping the horse at a walk.   No. 2½ is shut up
for the season. . . . Slope now becomes steep
as a stairway, and further riding would be dangerous.   Alight and make ready for the climb.
Cold wind blowing so strongly that I have to tie
on my hat tightly.   One of the gōriki unwinds
from about his waist a long stout cotton girdle,
and giving me one end to hold, passes the other
over his shoulder for the pull.   Then he proceeds
over the sand at an angle, with a steady short
step, and I follow; the other guide keeping
closely behind me to provide against any slip.

There is nothing very difficult about this climbing, except the weariness of walking through
sand and cinders : it is like walking over dunes.
. . . We mount by zigzags.   The sand moves
with the wind; and I have a slightly nervous
sense — the feeling only, not the perception ; for
I keep my eyes on the sand, — of height growing

above depth. . . . Have to watch my steps carefully, and to use my staff constantly, as the slant is now very steep. . . . We are in a white fog, — passing through clouds! Even if I wished to look back, I could see nothing through this vapor; but I have not the least wish to look back. The wind has suddenly ceased — cut off, perhaps, by a ridge; and there is a silence that I remember from West Indian days: the Peace of High Places. It is broken only by the crunching of the ashes beneath our feet. I can distinctly hear my heart beat. . . . The guide tells me that I stoop too much, — orders me to walk upright, and always in stepping to put down the heel first. I do this, and find it relieving. But climbing through this tiresome mixture of ashes and sand begins to be trying. I am perspiring and panting. The guide bids me keep my honorable mouth closed, and breathe only through my honorable nose.

We are out of the fog again. . . . All at once I perceive above us, at a little distance, something like a square hole in the face of the mountain, — a door! It is the door of the third station, — a wooden hut half-buried in black

drift. . . . How delightful to squat again, —
even in a blue cloud of wood-smoke and under
smoke-blackened rafters ! Time, 8:30 a. m.
Height, 7,085 feet.

In spite of the wood-smoke the station is com-
fortable enough inside ; there are clean mattings
and even kneeling-cushions. No windows, of
course, nor any other opening than the door ;
for the building is half-buried in the flank of the
mountain. We lunch. . . . The station-keeper
tells us that recently a student walked from
Gotemba to the top of the mountain and back
again — in geta ! Geta are heavy wooden sandals, or clogs, held to the foot only by a thong
passing between the great and the second toe.
The feet of that student must have been made
of steel !

Having rested, I go out to look around. Far
below white clouds are rolling over the landscape
in huge fluffy wreaths. Above the hut, and
actually trickling down over it, the sable cone
soars to the sky. But the amazing sight is the
line of the monstrous slope to the left, — a line
that now shows no curve whatever, but shoots
down below the clouds, and up to the gods only

know where (for I cannot see the end of it),
straight as a tightened bowstring. The right flank
is rocky and broken. But as for the left, — I
never dreamed it possible that a line so absolutely
straight and smooth, and extending for so enormous a distance at such an amazing angle, could
exist even in a volcano. That stupendous pitch
gives me a sense of dizziness, and a totally unfamiliar feeling of wonder. Such regularity appears unnatural, frightful; seems even artificial,
— but artificial upon a superhuman and demo-
niac scale. I imagine that to fall thence from
above would be to fall for leagues. Absolutely
nothing to take hold of. But the gōriki assure
me that there is no danger on that slope: it is all
soft sand.

IV

Though drenched with perspiration by the exer-
tion of the first climb, I am already dry, and cold.
. . . Up again. . . . The ascent is at first through
ashes and sand as before; but presently large stones
begin to mingle with the sand; and the way is
always growing steeper. . . . I constantly slip.

There is nothing firm, nothing resisting to stand upon: loose stones and cinders roll down at every step. . . . If a big lava-block were to detach itself from above! . . . In spite of my helpers and of the staff, I continually slip, and am all in perspiration again. Almost every stone that I tread upon turns under me. How is it that no stone ever turns under the feet of the gōriki? *They* never slip, — never make a false step, — never seem less at ease than they would be in walking over a matted floor. Their small brown broad feet always poise upon the shingle at exactly the right angle. They are heavier men than I; but they move lightly as birds. . . . Now I have to stop for rest every half-a-dozen steps. . . . The line of broken straw sandals follows the zigzags we take. . . . At last — at last another door in the face of the mountain. Enter the fourth station, and fling myself down upon the mats. Time, 10:30 a. m. Height, only 7,937 feet; — yet it seemed such a distance!

Off again. . . . Way worse and worse. . . . Feel a new distress due to the rarefaction of the air. Heart beating as in a high fever. . . . Slope has become very rough. It is no longer soft ashes

and sand mixed with stones, but stones only, —
fragments of lava, lumps of pumice, scoriæ of
every sort, all angled as if freshly broken with a
hammer. All would likewise seem to have been
expressly shaped so as to turn upside-down when
trodden upon. Yet I must confess that they never
turn under the feet of the gōriki. . . . The cast-
off sandals strew the slope in ever-increasing numbers. . . . But for the gōriki I should have had
ever so many bad tumbles: they cannot prevent
me from slipping; but they never allow me to
fall. Evidently I am not fitted to climb mountains. . . . Height, 8,659 feet — but the fifth
station is shut up! Must keep zigzaging on to
the next. Wonder how I shall ever be able to
reach it! . . . And there are people still alive
who have climbed Fuji three and four times, *for
pleasure!* . . . Dare not look back. See nothing but the black stones always turning under me,
and the bronzed feet of those marvellous gōriki
who never slip, never pant, and never perspire.
. . . Staff begins to hurt my hand. . . . Gōriki
push and pull: it is shameful of me, I know, to
give them so much trouble. . . . Ah! sixth station! — may all the myriads of the gods bless my
gōriki! Time, 2:07 p.m. Height, 9,317 feet.

Resting, 1 gaze through the doorway at the abyss below. The land is now dimly visible only through rents in a prodigious wilderness of white clouds; and within these rents everything looks almost black. . . . The horizon has risen frightfully, — has expanded monstrously. . . . My gōriki warn me that the summit is still miles away. I have been too slow. We must hasten upward.

Certainly the zigzag is steeper than before. . . . With the stones now mingle angular rocks; and we sometimes have to flank queer black bulks that look like basalt. . . . On the right rises, out of sight, a jagged black hideous ridge, — an ancient lava-stream. The line of the left slope still shoots up, straight as a bow-string. . . . Wonder if the way will become any steeper; — doubt whether it can possibly become any rougher. Rocks dislodged by my feet roll down soundlessly; — I am afraid to look after them. Their noiseless vanishing gives me a sensation like the sensation of falling in dreams. . . .

There is a white gleam overhead — the lowermost verge of an immense stretch of snow. . . . Now we are skirting a snow-filled gully, — the

lowermost of those white patches which, at first
sight of the summit this morning, seemed scarcely
an inch long. It will take an hour to pass it. . . .
A guide runs forward, while I rest upon my staff,
and returns with a large ball of snow. What
curious snow! Not flaky, soft, white snow, but
a mass of transparent globules, — exactly like
glass beads. I eat some, and find it deliciously
refreshing. . . . The seventh station is closed.
How shall I get to the eighth? . . . Happily,
breathing has become less difficult. . . . The
wind is upon us again, and black dust with it.
The gōriki keep close to me, and advance with
caution. . . . I have to stop for rest at every turn
on the path; — cannot talk for weariness. . . .
I do not feel; — I am much too tired to feel. . . .
How I managed it, I do not know; — but I have
actually got to the eighth station! Not for
a thousand millions of dollars will I go one step
further to-day. Time, 4:40 p. m. Height, 10,693
feet.

V

It is much too cold here for rest without winter clothing; and now I learn the worth of the heavy robes provided by the guides. The robes are blue, with big white Chinese characters on the back, and are padded thickly as bedquilts; but they feel light; for the air is really like the frosty breath of February. . . . A meal is preparing; — I notice that charcoal at this elevation acts in a refractory manner, and that a fire can be maintained only by constant attention. . . . Cold and fatigue sharpen appetite: we consume a surprising quantity of *Zō-sui*, — rice boiled with eggs and a little meat. By reason of my fatigue and of the hour, it has been decided to remain here for the night.

Tired as I am, I cannot but limp to the doorway to contemplate the amazing prospect. From within a few feet of the threshold, the ghastly slope of rocks and cinders drops down into a prodigious disk of clouds miles beneath us, — clouds of countless forms, but mostly wreathings and fluffy pilings; — and the whole huddling mass,

reaching almost to the horizon, is blinding white
under the sun. (By the Japanese, this tremendous
cloud-expanse is well named *Wata-no-Umi*, "the
Sea of Cotton.") The horizon itself — enormously risen, phantasmally expanded — seems half-
way up above the world : a wide luminous belt
ringing the hollow vision. Hollow, I call it, because extreme distances below the sky-line are
sky-colored and vague, — so that the impression
you receive is not of being on a point under a
vault, but of being upon a point rising into a stupendous blue sphere, of which this huge horizon
would represent the equatorial zone. To turn
away from such a spectacle is not possible. I
watch and watch until the dropping sun changes
the colors, — turning the Sea of Cotton into a
Fleece of Gold. Half-round the horizon a yellow
glory grows and burns. Here and there beneath
it, through cloudrifts, colored vaguenesses define :
I now see golden water, with long purple head-
lands reaching into it, with ranges of violet peaks
thronging behind it ; — these glimpses curiously
resembling portions of a tinted topographical map.
Yet most of the landscape is pure delusion. Even
my guides, with their long experience and their
eagle-sight, can scarcely distinguish the real from

the unreal; — for the blue and purple and violet clouds moving under the Golden Fleece, exactly mock the outlines and the tones of distant peaks and capes: you can detect what is vapor only by its slowly shifting shape. . . . Brighter and brighter glows the gold. Shadows come from the west, — shadows flung by cloud-pile over cloud-pile; and these, like evening shadows upon snow, are violaceous blue. . . . Then orange-tones appear in the horizon; then smouldering crimson. And now the greater part of the Fleece of Gold has changed to cotton again, — white cotton mixed with pink. . . . Stars thrill out. The cloud-waste uniformly whitens; — thickening and packing to the horizon. The west glooms. Night rises; and all things darken except that wondrous unbroken world-round of white, — the Sea of Cotton.

The station-keeper lights his lamps, kindles a fire of twigs, prepares our beds. Outside it is bitterly cold, and, with the fall of night, becoming colder. Still I cannot turn away from that astounding vision. . . . Countless stars now flicker and shiver in the blue-black sky. Nothing whatever of the material world remains visible, except the

black slope of the peak before my feet. The
enormous cloud-disk below continues white; but
to all appearance it has become a liquidly level
white, without forms, — a white flood. It is no
longer the Sea of Cotton. It is a Sea of Milk,
the Cosmic Sea of ancient Indian legend, — and
always self-luminous, as with ghostly quickenings.

VI

Squatting by the wood fire, I listen to the gōriki
and the station-keeper telling of strange happen-
ings on the mountain. One incident discussed I
remember reading something about in a Tōkyō
paper: I now hear it retold by the lips of a man
who figured in it as a hero.

A Japanese meteorologist named Nonaka, attempted last year the rash undertaking of passing
the winter on the summit of Fuji for purposes of
scientific study. It might not be difficult to winter upon the peak in a solid observatory furnished
with a good stove, and all necessary comforts;
but Nonaka could afford only a small wooden
hut, in which he would be obliged to spend the
cold season *without fire!* His young wife in-

sisted on sharing his labors and dangers. The couple began their sojourn on the summit toward the close of September. In midwinter news was brought to Gotemba that both were dying.

Relatives and friends tried to organize a rescue-party. But the weather was frightful; the peak was covered with snow and ice; the chances of death were innumerable; and the gōriki would not risk their lives. Hundreds of dollars could not tempt them. At last a desperate appeal was made to them as representatives of Japanese courage and hardihood: they were assured that to suffer a man of science to perish, without making even one plucky effort to save him, would disgrace the country; — they were told that the national honor was in their hands. This appeal brought forward two volunteers. One was a man of great strength and daring, nick-named by his fellow-guides, *Oni-guma*, "the Demon-Bear," the other was the elder of my gōriki. Both believed that they were going to certain destruction. They took leave of their friends and kindred, and drank with their families the farewell cup of water, — *midzu-no-sakazuki*, — in which those about to be separated by death pledge each other. Then, after having thickly wrapped themselves in cotton-wool, and made all possible preparation for ice climbing, they started, — taking with them a brave army-surgeon who had offered his services, without fee, for the rescue. After surmounting extraordinary difficulties, the party reached the hut; but the inmates refused to open! Nonaka protested that he would rather die than face the shame of failure in his undertaking; and his wife said that she had resolved to die with her husband. Partly by forcible, and partly by gentle means, the pair were restored to a better state of mind. The surgeon administered medicines and cordials; the patients, carefully wrapped up, were strapped to the backs of the guides; and the descent was begun. My gōriki, who carried the lady, believes that the gods helped him on the ice-slopes. More than once, all thought themselves lost; but they reached the foot of the mountain without one serious mishap. After weeks of careful nursing, the rash young couple were pronounced out of danger. The wife suffered less, and recovered more quickly, than the husband.

The gōriki have cautioned me not to venture outside during the night without calling them.

They will not tell me why; and their warning is peculiarly uncanny. From previous experiences during Japanese travel, I surmise that the danger implied is supernatural; but I feel that it would be useless to ask questions.

The door is closed and barred. I lie down between the guides, who are asleep in a moment, as I can tell by their heavy breathing. I cannot sleep immediately; — perhaps the fatigues and the surprises of the day have made me somewhat nervous. I look up at the rafters of the black roof, — at packages of sandals, bundles of wood, bundles of many indistinguishable kinds there stowed away or suspended, and making queer shadows in the lamplight. . . . It is terribly cold, even under my three quilts; and the sound of the wind outside is wonderfully like the sound of great surf, — a constant succession of bursting roars, each followed by a prolonged hiss. The hut, half buried under tons of rock and drift, does not move; but the sand does, and trickles down between the rafters; and small stones also move after each fierce gust, with a rattling just like the clatter of shingle in the pull of a retreating wave.

4. *a. m.* — Go out alone, despite last evening's warning, but keep close to the door. There is a great and icy blowing. The Sea of Milk is unchanged: it lies far below this wind. Over it the moon is dying. . . . The guides, perceiving my absence, spring up and join me. I am reproved for not having awakened them. They will not let me stay outside alone: so I turn in with them.

Dawn: a zone of pearl grows round the world. The stars vanish; the sky brightens. A wild sky, with dark wrack drifting at an enormous height. The Sea of Milk has turned again into Cotton,— and there are wide rents in it. The desolation of the black slope, — all the ugliness of slaggy rock and angled stone, again defines. . . . Now the cotton becomes disturbed ; — it is breaking up. A yellow glow runs along the east like the glare of a wind-blown fire. . . . Alas ! I shall not be among the fortunate mortals able to boast of viewing from Fuji the first lifting of the sun ! Heavy clouds have drifted across the horizon at the point where he should rise. . . . Now I know that he has risen ; because the upper edges of those purple rags of cloud are burning like charcoal. But I have been so disappointed !

More and more luminous the hollow world. League-wide heapings of cottony cloud roll apart. Fearfully far-away there is a light of gold upon water : the sun here remains viewless, but the ocean sees him. It is not a flicker, but a burnished glow ; — at such a distance ripplings are invisible. . . . Further and further scattering, the clouds unveil a vast grey and blue landscape ; — hundreds and hundreds of miles throng into vision at once. On the right I distinguish Tōkyō bay, and Kamakura, and the holy island of Enoshima (no bigger than the dot over this letter " i ") ; — on the left the wilder Suruga coast, and the blue-toothed promontory of Idzu, and the place of the fishing-village where I have been summering, — the merest pin-point in that tinted dream of hill and shore. Rivers appear but as sun-gleams on spider-threads ; — fishing-sails are white dust clinging to the grey-blue glass of the sea. And the picture alternately appears and vanishes while the clouds drift and shift across it, and shape themselves into spectral islands and mountains and valleys of all Elysian colors. . .

VII

6 : 40 *a. m.* — Start for the top. . . . Hardest
and roughest stage of the journey, through a wilderness of lava-blocks. The path zigzags between ugly masses that project from the slope
like black teeth. The trail of cast-away sandals
is wider than ever. . . . Have to rest every few
minutes. . . . Reach another long patch of the
snow that looks like glass-beads, and eat some.
The next station — a half-station — is closed ;
and the ninth has ceased to exist. . . . A sudden
fear comes to me, not of the ascent, but of the
prospective descent by a route which is too steep
even to permit of comfortably sitting down. But
the guides assure me that there will be no difficulty, and that most of the return-journey will
be by another way, — over the interminable level
which I wondered at yesterday, — nearly all soft
sand, with very few stones. It is called the
bashiri (" glissade ") ; and we are to descend at
a run ! . . .

All at once a family of field-mice scatter out
from under my feet in panic ; and the gōriki behind me catches one, and gives it to me. I hold

3

the tiny shivering life for a moment to examine it, and set it free again. These little creatures have very long pale noses. How do they live in this waterless desolation, — and at such an altitude, — especially in the season of snow? For we are now at a height of more than eleven thousand feet! The gōriki say that the mice find roots growing under the stones. . . .

Wilder and steeper; — for me, at least, the climbing is sometimes on all fours. There are barriers which we surmount with the help of ladders. There are fearful places with Buddhist names, such as the *Sai-no-Kawara,* or Dry Bed of the River of Souls, — a black waste strewn with heaps of rock, like those stone-piles which, in Buddhist pictures of the underworld, the ghosts of children build. . . .

Twelve thousand feet, and something, — the top! Time, 8:20 a. m. . . . Stone huts; Shintō shrine with tōrii; icy well, called the Spring of Gold; stone tablet bearing a Chinese poem and the design of a tiger; rough walls of lava-blocks round these things, — possibly for protection against the wind. Then the huge dead crater, — probably between a quarter of a mile and half-a-mile wide, but shallowed up to within three or four hundred feet of the verge by volcanic detritus, — a cavity horrible even in the tones of its yellow crumbling walls, streaked and stained with every hue of scorching. I perceive that the trail of straw sandals ends *in* the crater. Some hideous over-hanging cusps of black lava — like the broken edges of a monstrous cicatrix — project on two sides several hundred feet above the opening; but I certainly shall not take the trouble to climb them. Yet these, — seen through the haze of a hundred miles, — through the soft illusion of blue spring-weather, — appear as the opening snowy petals of the bud of the Sacred Lotos! . . . No spot in this world can be more horrible, more atrociously dismal, than the cindered tip of the Lotos as you stand upon it.

But the view — the view for a hundred leagues, — and the light of the far faint dreamy world, — and the fairy vapors of morning, — and the marvellous wreathings of cloud: all this, and only this, consoles me for the labor and the pain. . . . Other pilgrims, earlier climbers, — poised upon the highest crag, with faces turned to the tremendous East, — are clapping their hands in Shintō prayer, saluting the mighty

Day. . . . The immense poetry of the moment
enters into me with a thrill. I know that the
colossal vision before me has already become a
memory ineffaceable, — a memory of which no
luminous detail can fade till the hour when
thought itself must fade, and the dust of these
eyes be mingled with the dust of the myriad
million eyes that also have looked, in ages forgotten before my birth, from the summit supreme
of Fuji to the Rising of the Sun.

Insect-Musicians

Insect-Musicians

❧

Mushi yo mushi,
Naïté ingwa ga
Tsukuru nara?

"O insect, insect!—think you that Karma can be exhausted by song?"—*Japanese poem.*

I

IF you ever visit Japan, be sure to go to at least
one temple-festival,—*en-nichi*. The festival ought to be seen at night, when everything shows to the best advantage in the glow of
countless lamps and lanterns. Until you have
had this experience, you cannot know what Japan
is,—you cannot imagine the real charm of queer-
ness and prettiness, the wonderful blending of
grotesquery and beauty, to be found in the life
of the common people.

In such a night you will probably let yourself
drift awhile with the stream of sight-seers through

dazzling lanes of booths full of toys indescribable
— dainty puerilities, fragile astonishments, laugh-
ter-making oddities ; — you will observe represen-
tations of demons, gods, and goblins ; — you will
be startled by *mandō* — immense lantern-trans-
parencies, with monstrous faces painted upon
them ; — you will have glimpses of jugglers,
acrobats, sword-dancers, fortune-tellers ; — you
will hear everywhere, above the tumult of voices,
a ceaseless blowing of flutes and booming of
drums.   All this may not be worth stopping for.
But presently, I am almost sure, you will pause
in your promenade to look at a booth illuminated
like a magic-lantern, and stocked with tiny wooden
cages out of which an incomparable shrilling proceeds.   The booth is the booth of a vendor of
singing-insects ; and the storm of noise is made
by the insects.   The sight is curious ; and a
foreigner is nearly always attracted by it.

But having satisfied his momentary curiosity,
the foreigner usually goes on his way with the idea
that he has been inspecting nothing more remarkable than a particular variety of toys for children.
He might easily be made to understand that the
insect-trade of Tōkyō alone represents a yearly
value of thousands of dollars ; but he would

certainly wonder if assured that the insects themselves are esteemed for the peculiar character of
the sounds which they make. It would not be
easy to convince him that in the æsthetic life of a
most refined and artistic people, these insects hold
a place not less important or well-deserved than
that occupied in Western civilization by our
thrushes, linnets, nightingales and canaries. What
stranger could suppose that a literature one thousand years old, — a literature full of curious and
delicate beauty, — exists upon the subject of these
short-lived insect-pets?

The object of the present paper is, by elucidat-
ing these facts, to show how superficially our
travellers might unconsciously judge the most
interesting details of Japanese life. But such
misjudgments are as natural as they are inevit-
able. Even with the kindest of intentions it
is impossible to estimate correctly at sight anything of the extraordinary in Japanese custom, —
because the extraordinary nearly always relates
to feelings, beliefs, or thoughts about which a
stranger cannot know anything.

Before proceeding further, let me observe that
the domestic insects of which I am going to

speak, are mostly night-singers, and must not be confounded with the *semi* (cicadæ), mentioned in former essays of mine. I think that the cicadæ, — even in a country so exceptionally rich as is Japan in musical insects, — are wonderful melodists in their own way. But the Japanese find as much difference between the notes of night-insects and of cicadæ as we find between those of larks and sparrows; and they relegate their cicadæ to the vulgar place of chatterers. *Semi* are therefore never caged. The national liking for caged insects does not mean a liking for mere noise; and the note of every insect in public favor must possess either some rhythmic charm, or some mimetic quality celebrated in poetry or legend. The same fact is true of the Japanese liking for the chant of frogs. It would be a mistake to suppose that all kinds of frogs are considered musical; but there are particular species of very small frogs having sweet notes; and these are caged and petted.

Of course, in the proper meaning of the word, insects do not *sing*; but in the following pages I may occasionally employ the terms "singer" and "singing-insect," — partly because of their convenience, and partly because of their correspondence with the language used by Japanese insect-dealers and poets, describing the " voices " of such creatures.

II

There are many curious references in the old Japanese classic literature to the custom of keeping musical insects. For example in the chapter entitled *Nowaki*[1] of the famous novel " Genji Monogatari," written in the latter part of the tenth century by the Lady Murasaki-Shikibu, it is stated : " The maids were ordered to descend to the garden, and give some water to the insects." But the first definite mention of cages for singing-insects would appear to be the following passage from a work entitled *Chomon-Shū :* — " On the twelfth day of the eighth month of the second year of Kaho [1095 A. D.], the Emperor ordered his pages and chamberlains to go to Sagano and find some insects. The Emperor gave them a

[1] *Nowaki* is the name given to certain destructive storms usually occurring toward the end of autumn. All the chapters of the Genji Monogatari have remarkably poetical and effective titles. There is an English translation, by Mr. Kenchō Suyematsu, of the first seventeen chapters.

cage of network of bright purple thread. All,
even the head-chaplain and his attendants, taking
horses from the Right and the Left Imperial
Mews, then went on horseback to hunt for
insects.   Tokinori Ben, at that time holding the
office of *Kurando*,[1] proposed to the party as they
rode toward Sagano, a subject for poetical composition.   The subject was, *Looking for insects
in the fields*.   On reaching Sagano, the party
dismounted, and walked in various directions
for a distance of something more than ten *chō*,[2]
and sent their attendants to catch the insects.
In the evening they returned to the palace.
They put into the cage some *hagi*[3] and *ominameshi* [for the insects].   The cage was respectfully presented to the Empress.   There was *saké*-
drinking in the palace that evening ; and many
poems were composed.   The Empress and her
court-ladies joined in the making of the poems."

This would appear to be the oldest Japanese
record of an insect-hunt, — though the amuse-

[1] The Kurando, or Kurōdo, was an official intrusted with
the care of the imperial records.

[2] A *chō* is about one-fifteenth of a mile.

[3] *Hagi* is the name commonly given to the bush-clover.
Ominameshi is the common term for the *valeriana officinalis*.

ment may have been invented earlier than the
period of Kaho. By the seventeenth century
it seems to have become a popular diversion;
and night-hunts were in vogue as much as day-
hunts. In the *Teikoku Bunshū*, or collected works
of the poet Teikoku, who died during the second
year of Shōwō (1653), there has been preserved
one of the poet's letters which contains a very
interesting passage on the subject. " Let us go
insect-hunting this evening," — writes the poet to
his friend. " It is true that the night will be very
dark, since there is no moon; and it may seem
dangerous to go out. But there are many people
now going to the graveyards every night, because
the Bon festival is approaching [1]; — therefore the
way to the fields will not be lonesome for us. I
have prepared many lanterns; — so the *hata-ori*,
matsumushi, and other insects will probably come
to the lanterns in great number."

It would also seem that the trade of insect-
seller (*mushiya*) existed in the seventeenth century; for in a diary of that time, known as

[1] That is to say, there are now many people who go
every night to the graveyards, to decorate and prepare the
graves before the great Festival of the Dead.

the Diary of Kikaku, the writer speaks of his dis-
appointment at not finding any insect-dealers in
Yedo, — tolerably good evidence that he had met
such persons elsewhere. " On the thirteenth day
of the sixth month of the fourth year of Teikyo
[1687], I went out," he writes, "to look for
kirigirisu-sellers. I searched for them in Yot-
suya, in Kōjimachi, in Hongō, in Yushimasa, and
in both divisions of Kanda-Sudamachō[1]; but I
found none."

As we shall presently see, the *kirigirisu* was
not sold in Tōkyō until about one hundred and
twenty years later.

But long before it became the fashion to keep
singing-insects, their music had been celebrated
by poets as one of the æsthetic pleasures of
the autumn.   There are charming references to
singing-insects in poetical collections made during the tenth century, and doubtless containing
many compositions of a yet earlier period.   And
just as places famous for cherry, plum, or other
blossoming trees, are still regularly visited every
year by thousands and tens of thousands, merely

[1] Most of these names survive in the appellations of
well-known districts of the present Tōkyō.

for the delight of seeing the flowers in their seasons, — so in ancient times city-dwellers made
autumn excursions to country-districts simply for
the pleasure of hearing the chirruping choruses
of crickets and of locusts, — the night-singers
especially. Centuries ago places were noted as
pleasure-resorts solely because of this melodious
attraction ; — such were Musashino (now Tōkyō),
Yatano in the province of Echizen, and Mano in
the province of Ōmi. Somewhat later, probably,
people discovered that each of the principal species
of singing-insects haunted by preference some particular locality, where its peculiar chanting could
be heard to the best advantage ; and eventually
no less than eleven places became famous throughout Japan for different kinds of insect-music.

The best places to hear the *matsumushi*
were : —

(1) Arashiyama, near Kyōto, in the province
of Yamashiro ;

(2) Sumiyoshi, in the province of Settsu ;

(3) Miyagino, in the province of Mutsu.

The best places to hear the *suzumushi* were : —

(4) Kagura-ga-Oka, in Yamashiro ;

(5) Ogura-yama, in Yamashiro ;

(6) Suzuka-yama, in Isé ;
(7) Narumi, in Owari.

The best places to hear the *kirigirisu* were : —

(8) Sagano, in Yamashiro ;
(9) Takeda-no-Sato, in Yamashiro ;
(10) Tatsuta-yama, in Yamato ;
(11) Ono-no-Shinowara, in Ōmi.

Afterwards, when the breeding and sale of singing-insects became a lucrative industry, the custom of going into the country to hear them gradually went out of fashion. But even to-day city-dwellers, when giving a party, will sometimes place cages of singing-insects among the garden-shrubbery, so that the guests may enjoy not only the music of the little creatures, but also those memories or sensations of rural peace which such music evokes.

III

The regular trade in musical insects is of comparatively modern origin. In Tōkyō its beginnings date back only to the Kwansei era (1789–1800), — at which period, however, the

capital of the Shōgunate was still called Yedo.
A complete history of the business was recently
placed in my hands, — a history partly compiled
from old documents, and partly from traditions
preserved in the families of several noted insect-
merchants of the present day.

The founder of the Tōkyō trade was an itinerant foodseller named Chūzō, originally from
Echigo, who settled in the Kanda district of the
city in the latter part of the eighteenth century.
One day, while making his usual rounds, it occurred to him to capture a few of the *suzumushi*,
or bell-insects, then very plentiful in the Negishi
quarter, and to try the experiment of feeding
them at home. They throve and made music in
confinement ; and several of Chūzō's neighbors,
charmed by their melodious chirruping, asked to
be supplied with *suzumushi* for a consideration.
From this accidental beginning, the demand for
suzumushi grew rapidly to such proportions that
the foodseller at last decided to give up his
former calling and to become an insect-seller.

Chūzō only caught and sold insects : he never
imagined that it would be more profitable to
breed them. But the fact was presently discov-

ered by one of his customers, — a man named
Kirayama, then in the service of the Lord
Aoyama Shimodzuké-no-Kami.   Kiriyama had
bought from Chūzō several *suzumushi*, which
were kept and fed in a jar half-filled with moist
clay.   They died in the cold season; but during
the following summer Kiriyama was agreeably
surprised to find the jar newly peopled with a
number of young ones, evidently born from eggs
which the first prisoners had left in the clay.   He
fed them carefully, and soon had the pleasure,
my chronicler says, of hearing them " begin to
sing in small voices."   Then he resolved to make
some experiments; and, aided by Chūzō, who
furnished the males and females, he succeeded in
breeding not only *suzumushi*, but three other
kinds of singing-insects also, — *kantan, matsumushi,* and *kutsuwamushi*.   He discovered, at the
same time, that, by keeping his jars in a warm
room, the insects could be hatched considerably
in advance of the natural season.   Chūzō sold
for Kiriyama these home-bred singers; and both
men found the new undertaking profitable beyond
expectation.

The example set by Kiriyama was imitated by
a *tabiya*, or stocking-maker named Yasubei (com-

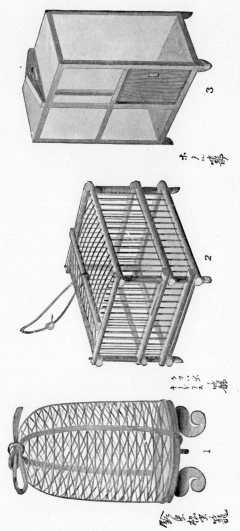

1. A FORM OF INSECT CAGE. 2. CAGE FOR LARGE MUSICAL INSECTS. — *Kirigirisu*, *Kutsuwamushi*, etc.

3. CAGE FOR SMALL MUSICAL INSECTS, OR FIRE-FLIES

monly known as Tabiya Yasubei by reason of his
calling), who lived in Kanda-ku. Yasubei likewise made careful study of the habits of singing-
insects, with a view to their breeding and nourish-
ment; and he soon found himself able to carry
on a small trade in them. Up to that time the
insects sold in Yedo would seem to have been
kept in jars or boxes: Yasubei conceived the
idea of having special cages manufactured for
them. A man named Kondō, vassal to the Lord
Kamei of Honjō-ku, interested himself in the
matter, and made a number of pretty little cages
which delighted Yasubei, and secured a large
order from him. The new invention found public favor at once; and Kondō soon afterwards
established the first manufactory of insect-cages.

The demand for singing-insects increased from
this time so rapidly, that Chūzō soon found it
impossible to supply all his would-be customers
directly. He therefore decided to change his
business to wholesale trade, and to sell to retail
dealers only. To meet orders, he purchased
largely from peasants in the suburbs and elsewhere. Many persons were employed by him;
and Yasubei and others paid him a fixed annual
sum for sundry rights and privileges.

Some time after this Yasubei became the first itinerant-vendor of singing-insects. He walked through the streets crying his wares; but hired a number of servants to carry the cages. Tradition says that while going his rounds he used to wear a *katabira*[1] made of a much-esteemed silk stuff called *sukiya*, together with a fine Hakata-girdle; and that this elegant way of dressing proved of much service to him in his business.

Two men, whose names have been preserved, soon entered into competition with Yasubei. The first was Yasakura Yasuzō, of Honjō-ku, by previous occupation a *sahainin*, or property-agent. He prospered, and became widely known as Mushi-Yasu, — "Yasu-the-Insect-Man." His success encouraged a former fellow-*sahainin*, Genbei of Uyeno, to go into the same trade. Genbei likewise found insect-selling a lucrative occupation, and earned for himself the sobriquet of Mushi-Gen, by which he is yet remembered.

---

[1] *Katabira* is a name given to many kinds of light textures used for summer-robes. The material is usually hemp, but sometimes, as in the case referred to here, of fine silk. Some of these robes are transparent, and very beautiful. — Hakata, in Kyūshū, is still famous for the silk girdles made there. The fabric is very heavy and strong.

His descendants in Tōkyō to-day are *amé*[1]-manu-
facturers; but they still carry on the hereditary
insect-business during the summer and autumn
months; and one of the firm was kind enough
to furnish me with many of the facts recorded in
this little essay.

Chūzō, the father and founder of all this curious
commerce, died without children; and sometime
in the period of Bunsei (1818–1829) his business
was taken over by a distant relative named Yamasaki Seïchirō. To Chūzō's business, Yamasaki
joined his own, — that of a toy-merchant. About
the same time a law was passed limiting the
number of insect-dealers in the municipality to
thirty-six. The thirty-six then formed themselves into a guild, called the Ōyama-Kō (" Ōyama Society"), having for patron the divinity
Sekison-Sama of the mountain Ōyama in Sagami Province.[2] But in business the association

---

[1] *Amé* is a nutritive gelatinous extract obtained from
wheat and other substances. It is sold in many forms — as
candy, as a syrupy liquid resembling molasses, as a sweet
hot drink, as a solid jelly. Children are very fond of it.
Its principal element is starch-sugar.

[2] Ōyama mountain in Sagami is a great resort of
Pilgrims. There is a celebrated temple there, dedicated
to Iwanaga-Himé (" Long-Rock Princess "), sister of the

was known as the Yedō-Mushi-Kō, or Yedo
Insect-Company.

It is not until after this consolidation of the
trade that we hear of the *kirigirisu*, — the same
musical insect which the poet Kikaku had vainly
tried to buy in the city in 1687, — being sold
in Yedo. One of the guild known as Mushiya
Kojirō ("Kojirō the Insect-Merchant"), who did
business in Honjō-Ku, returning to the city after
a short visit to his native place in Kadzusa,
brought back with him a number of *kirigirisu*,
which he sold at a good profit. Although long
famous elsewhere, these insects had never before
been sold in Yedo.

"When Midzu Echizen-no-Kami," says the
chronicle, "became *machi-bugyō* (or chief mag-
istrate) of Yedo, the law limiting the number
of insect-dealers to thirty-six, was abolished."
Whether the guild was subsequently dissolved
the chronicle fails to mention.

Kiriyama, the first to breed singing-insects artificially, had, like Chūzō, built up a prosperous
trade. He left a son, Kaméjirō, who was adopted
into the family of one Yumoto, living in Waséda,

beautiful Goddess of Fuji.   Sekison-San is a popular name
both for the divinity and for the mountain itself.

Ushigomé-ku.   Kaméjirō brought with him to the
Yumoto family the valuable secrets of his father's
occupation ; and the Yumoto family is still celebrated in the business of insect breeding.

To-day the greatest insect-merchant in Tōkyō
is said to be Kawasumi Kanésaburō, of Samon-
chō in Yotsuya-ku.   A majority of the lesser
dealers obtain their autumn stock from him.   But
the insects bred artificially, and sold in summer,
are mostly furnished by the Yumoto house.   Other
noted dealers are Mushi-Sei, of Shitaya-ku, and
Mushi-Toku, of Asakusa.   These buy insects
caught in the country, and brought to the city by
the peasants.   The wholesale dealers supply both
insects and cages to multitudes of itinerant vendors
who do business in the neighborhood of the parish-
temples during the *en-nichi*, or religious festivals,
— especially after dark.   Almost every night of
the year there are *en-nichi* in some quarter of the
capital ; and the insect-sellers are rarely idle during the summer and autumn months.

Perhaps the following list of current Tōkyō
prices[1] for singing-insects may interest the
reader : —

[1] Prices of the year 1897.

Suzumushi	. . . . 3 sen 5 rin, to 4 sen.
Matsumushi	. . . . 4 " . . . . 5 "
Kantan	. . . . . . 10 " . . . . 12 "
Kin-hibari	. . . . . 10 " . . . . 12 "
Kusa-hibari	. . . . 10 " . . . . 12 "
Kuro-hibari	. . . . . 8 " . . . . 12 "
Kutsuwamushi	. . . 10 " . . . . 15 "
Yamato-suzu	. . . . 8 " . . . . 12 "
Kirigirisu	. . . . . 12 " . . . . 15 "
Emma-kōrogi	. . . . 5 "
Kanétataki	. . . . . 12 "
Umaoi	. . . . . . 10 "

These prices, however, rule only during the
busy period of the insect trade. In May and the
latter part of June the prices are high, — for only
artificially bred insects are then in the market. In
July *kirigirisu* brought from the country will
sell as low as one sen. The *kantan, kusa-hibari*,
and *Yamato-suzu* sell sometimes as low as two
sen. In August the *Emma-kōrogi* can be bought
even at the rate of ten for one sen ; and in September the *kuro-hibari, kanétataki*, and *umaoi*
sell for one or one and a half sen each. But
there is little variation at any season in the prices
of *suzumushi* and of *matsumushi*. These are
never very dear, but never sell at less than three
sen ; and there is always a demand for them. The
suzumushi is the most popular of all ; and the

greater part of the profits annually made in the insect-trade is said to be gained on the sale of this insect.

IV

As will be seen from the foregoing price-list, twelve varieties of musical insects are sold in Tōkyō. Nine can be artificially bred, — namely the *suzumushi, matsumushi, kirigirisu, kantan, kutsuwamushi, Emma-kōrogi, kin-hibari, kusa-hibari* (also called *Asa-suzu*), and the *Yamato-suzu,* or *Yoshino-suzu.* Three varieties, I am

KANÉTATAKI ("THE BELL-RINGER") (*natural size*).

told, are not bred for sale, but captured for the market: these are the *kanétataki, umaoi* or *bataori,* and *kuro-hibari.* But a considerable number of all the insects annually offered for sale, are caught in their native haunts.

The night-singers are, with few exceptions, easily taken. They are captured with the help of lanterns. Being quickly attracted by light, they approach the lanterns; and when near enough to be observed, they can readily be covered with nets or little baskets. Males and females are usually secured at the same time, for the creatures move about in couples. Only the males sing; but a certain number of females are always taken for breeding purposes. Males and females are kept in the same vessel only for breeding: they are never left together in a cage, because the male ceases to sing when thus mated, and will die in a short time after pairing.

The breeding pairs are kept in jars or other earthen vessels half-filled with moistened clay, and are supplied every day with fresh food. They do not live long: the male dies first, and the female survives only until her eggs have been laid. The young insects hatched from them, shed their skin in about forty days from birth, after which they grow more rapidly, and soon attain their full development. In their natural state these creatures are hatched a little before the

Doyō, or Period of Greatest Heat by the old
calendar, — that is to say, about the middle
of July; — and they begin to sing in October.
But when bred in a warm room, they are hatched
early in April; and, with careful feeding, they
can be offered for sale before the end of May.
When very young, their food is triturated and
spread for them upon a smooth piece of wood;
but the adults are usually furnished with unpre-
pared food, — consisting of parings of egg-plant,
melon-rind, cucumber-rind, or the soft interior
parts of the white onion. Some insects, however,
are specially nourished; — the *abura-kirigirisu*,
for example, being fed with sugar-water and
slices of musk-melon.

V

All the insects mentioned in the Tōkyō price-
list are not of equal interest; and several of the
names appear to refer only to different varieties
of one species, — though on this point I am not
positive. Some of the insects do not seem to
have yet been scientifically classed; and I am
no entomologist. But I can offer some general

notes on the more important among the little melodists, and free translations of a few out of the countless poems about them, — beginning with the *matsumushi*, which was celebrated in Japanese verse a thousand years ago :

Matsumushi.[1]

As ideographically written, the name of this creature signifies " pine-insect ; " but, as pronounced, it might mean also " waiting-insect," —

since the verb "*matsu*," " to wait," and the noun " *matsu*," " pine," have the same sound. It is chiefly upon this double meaning of the word as uttered that a host of Japanese poems about the *matsumushi* are

MATSUMUSHI (*slightly enlarged*). based. Some of these are very old, — dating back to the tenth century at least.

Although by no means a rare insect, the matsumushi is much esteemed for the peculiar clear-

---

[1] *Calyptotryphus Marmoratus.* (?)

ness and sweetness of its notes— (onomatopoetically rendered in Japanese by the syllables
chin-chirorīn, chin-chirorīn), — little silvery
shrillings which I can best describe as resembling
the sound of an electric bell heard from a distance. The matsumushi haunts pine-woods and
cryptomeria-groves, and makes its music at night.
It is a very small insect, with a dark-brown back,
and a yellowish belly.

Perhaps the oldest extant verses upon the
matsumushi are those contained in the *Kokinshū*,
— a famous anthology compiled in the year 905
by the court-poet Tsurayuki and several of his
noble friends. Here we first find that play on
the name of the insect as pronounced, which was
to be repeated in a thousand different keys by a
multitude of poets through the literature of more
than nine hundred years: —

> Aki no no ni
> Michi mo madoinu;
> Matsumushi no
> Koe suru kata ni
> Yadoya karamashi.

" In the autumn-fields I lose my way ; — perhaps
I might ask for lodging in the direction of the

cry of the waiting-insect; " — that is to say, " might sleep to-night in the grass where the insects are waiting for me." There is in the same work a much prettier poem on the matsumushi by Tsurayuki.

With dusk begins to cry the male of the Waiting-insect; — I, too, await my beloved, and, hearing, my longing grows.

The following poems on·the same insect are less ancient but not less interesting : —

Forever past and gone, the hour of the promised advent ! — Truly the Waiter's voice is a voice of sadness now !

Parting is sorrowful always, — even the parting with autumn !
O plaintive matsumushi, add not thou to my pain !

Always more clear and shrill, as the hush of the night grows deeper,
The Waiting-insect's voice; — and I that wait in the garden,
Feel enter into my heart the voice and the moon together.

Suzumushi.[1]

The name signifies " bell-insect; " but the bell of which the sound is thus referred to is a very small bell, or a bunch of little bells such as a Shinto priestess uses in the sacred dances. The

---

[1] *Homeogryllus Japonicus.*

suzumushi is a great favorite with insect-fanciers,
and is bred in great numbers for the market. In
the wild state it is found in many parts of Japan;
and at night the noise made by multitudes of
suzumushi in certain lonesome places might easily

be mistaken, — as
it has been by
myself more than
once, — for the
sound of rapids.
The Japanese de-
scription of the
insect as resem-

SUZUMUSHI (*slightly enlarged*).

bling "a watermelon seed" — the black kind —
is excellent. It is very small, with a black back,
and a white or yellowish belly. Its tintinnabula-
tion — *ri-i-i-i-in*, as the Japanese render the
sound — might easily be mistaken for the tinkling of a *suzu*. Both the *matsumushi* and the
suzumushi are mentioned in Japanese poems of
the period of Engi (901–922).

Some of the following poems on the suzumushi
are very old; others are of comparatively recent
date: —

Yes, my dwelling is old: weeds on the roof are growing; —
But the voice of the suzumushi — that will never be old!

To-day united in love, — we who can meet so rarely!
Hear how the insects ring! — their bells to our hearts keep
    time.

The tinkle of tiny bells, — the voices of suzumushi,
I hear in the autumn-dusk, — and think of the fields at home.

Even the moonshine sleeps on the dews of the garden-
    grasses;
Nothing moves in the night but the suzumushi's voice.

Heard in these alien fields, the voice of the suzumushi, —
Sweet in the evening-dusk, — sounds like the sound of
    home.

Vainly the suzumushi exhausts its powers of pleasing,
Always, the long night through, my tears continue to flow!

Hark to those tinkling tones, — the chant of the suzumushi!
— If a jewel of dew could sing, it would tinkle with such a
    voice!

Foolish-fond I have grown; — I feel for the suzumushi! —
In the time of the heavy rains, what will the creature do?

Hataori-mushi.

The *hataori* is a beautiful bright-green grass-
hopper, of very graceful shape. Two reasons
are given for its curious name, which signifies
"the Weaver." One is that, when held in a
particular way, the struggling gestures of the
creature resemble the movements of a girl weaving. The other reason is that its music seems to

imitate the sound of the reed and shuttle of a
hand-loom in operation, — *Ji-i-i-i* — *chon-chon!*
— *ji-i-i-i* — *chon-chon!*

There is a pretty folk-story about the origin
of the *hataori* and the *kirigirisu*, which used to
be told to Japanese children in former times. —
Long, long ago, says the tale, there were two
very dutiful daughters who supported their old
blind father by the labor of their hands. The
elder girl used to weave, and the younger to sew.
When the old blind father died at last, these good
girls grieved so much that they soon died also.
One beautiful morning, some creatures of a kind
never seen before were found making music
above the graves of the sisters. On the tomb
of the elder was a pretty green insect, producing
sounds like those made by a girl weaving, —
ji-i-i-i, chon-chon! ji-i-i-i, chon-chon! This
was the first *hataori-mushi*. On the tomb of
the younger sister was an insect which kept crying
out, " *Tsuzuré — sasé, sasé! — tsuzuré, tsuzuré
— sasé, sasé, sasé!* " (Torn clothes — patch,
patch them up! — torn clothes, torn clothes —
patch up, patch up, patch up!) This was the
first *kirigirisu*. Then everybody knew that the

5

spirits of the good sisters had taken those shapes.
Still every autumn they cry to wives and daughters to work well at the loom, and warn them to
repair the winter garments of the household
before the coming of the cold.

Such poems as I have been able to obtain about
the *hataori* consist of nothing more than pretty
fancies.   Two, of which I offer free renderings,
are ancient, — the first by Tsurayuki ; the second
by a poetess classically known as " Akinaka's
Daughter " : —

Weaving-insects I hear; and the fields, in their autumn-
      colors,
Seem of Chinese-brocade : — was this the weavers' work ?

Gossamer-threads are spread over the shrubs and grasses :
Weaving-insects I hear ; — do they weave with spider-silk ?

Umaoi.

The *umaoi* is sometimes confounded with the
hataori, which it much resembles.   But the true
umaoi — (called *junta* in Izumo) — is a shorter
and thicker insect than the *hataori ;* and has at
its tail a hook-shaped protuberance, which the
weaver-insect has not.   Moreover, there is some
difference in the sounds made by the two creatures.   The music of the umaoi is not " *ji-i-i-i,*

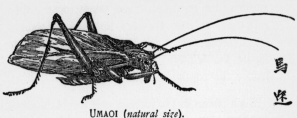

UMAOI (*natural size*).

— *chon-chon*," but, " *ʒu-i-in-tʒō !* — *ʒu-i-in-tʒō !* " — say the Japanese.

Kirigirisu.[1]

There are different varieties of this much-prized insect. The *abura-kirigirisu*, a day-singer, is a delicate creature, and must be carefully nourished in confinement. The *tachi-kirigirisu,* a night-singer, is more commonly found in the market. Captured *kirigirisu* sold in Tōkyō are mostly from the neighborhood of Itabashi, Niiso, and Todogawa ; and these, which fetch high prices, are considered the best. They are large vigorous insects, uttering very clear notes. From Kujiukuri in Kadzusa other and much cheaper *kirigirisu* are brought to the capital ; but these have a dis-agreeable odor, suffer from the attacks of a peculiar parasite, and are feeble musicians.

[1] *Locusta Japonica.* (?)

As stated elsewhere, the sounds made by the kirigirisu are said to resemble those of the Japanese words, " *Tsuzuré — sasé! sasé!* " (Torn clothes — patch up! patch up!); and a large proportion of the many poems written about the

KIRIGIRISU (*natural size*).

insect depend for interest upon ingenious but untranslatable allusions to those words.   I offer renderings therefore of only two poems on the *kirigirisu*, — the first by an unknown poet in the *Kokinshū*; the second by Tadafusa : —

O Kirigirisu ! when the clover changes color,
Are the nights then sad for you as for me that cannot
    sleep ?

O Kirigirisu ! cry not, I pray, so loudly !
Hearing, my sorrow grows, — and the autumn-night is
    long !

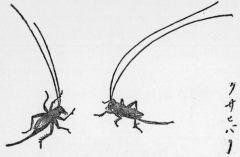

KUSA-HIBARI (*natural size*).

Kusa-hibari.

The *kusa-hibari,* or "Grass-Lark," — also called *Asa-suzu,* or "Morning-Bell;" *Yabu-suzu,* or "the Little Bell of the Bamboo-grove;" *Aki-kazė,* or "Autumn-Wind;" and *Ko-suzu-mushi,* or "the Child of the Bell-Insect," — is a day-singer. It is very small, — perhaps the smallest of the insect-choir, except the *Yamato-suzu.*

YAMATO-SUZU
("LITTLE-BELL OF YAMATO")
(*natural size*).

Kin-hibari.

The *kin-hibari*, or "Golden Lark" used to be found in great numbers about the neighborhood of the well-known Shinobazu-no-iké, — the great lotospond of Uyeno in Tōkyō; — but of late years it has become scarce there. The *kin-hibari*

KIN-HIBARI *natural size*).

now sold in the capital are brought from Todogawa and Shimura.

Kuro-hibari.

The *kuro-hibari*, or "Black Lark," is rather uncommon, and comparatively dear. It is caught in the country about Tōkyō, but is never bred.

KURO-HIBARI (*natural size*).

Kōrogi.

There are many varieties of this night-cricket, — called *kōrogi* from its music : — " *kiri-kiri-kiri-kiri! — kōro-kōro-kōro-kōro! — ghi-i-i-i-i-i!* "

One variety, the *ebi-kōrogi*, or "shrimp-kōrogi," does not make any sound. But the *uma-kōrogi*, or "horse-kōrogi;" the *Oni-kōrogi*, or "Demon-kōrogi;" and the *Emma-kōrogi*, or "Cricket-of-Emma [1] [King of the Dead]," are all good musicians. The color is blackish-brown, or

エンマコホロギ

EMMA-KŌROGI (*natural size*).

black; — the best singing-varieties have curious wavy markings on the wings.

An interesting fact regarding the *kōrogi* is that mention of it is made in the very oldest collection of Japanese poems known, — the *Manyōshu*, probably compiled about the middle of the eighth

[1] Sanscrit: *Yama*. Probably this name was given to the insect on account of its large staring eyes. Images of King Emma are always made with very big and awful eyes.

century. The following lines, by an unknown poet, which contain this mention, are therefore considerably more than eleven hundred years old : —

Niwa-kusa ni
Murasamé furité
Kōrogi no
Naku oto kikeba
Aki tsukinikeri.

エ
ン
ン
コ
ヲ
ロ
ギ

[" Showers have sprinkled the garden-grass. Hearing the sound of the crying of the kōrogi, I know that the autumn has come."]

EMMA-KŌROGI.

Kutsuwamushi.

There are several varieties of this extraordinary creature, — also called onomatopoetically *gatcha-gatcha*, — which is most provokingly described in dictionaries as " a kind of noisy cricket " ! The variety commonly sold in Tōkyō has a green back, and a yellowish-white abdomen; but there are also brown and reddish varieties. The *kut suwamushi* is difficult to capture, but easy to breed. As the *tsuku-tsuku-bōshi* is the most wonderful musician among the sun-loving cicadæ

KUTSUWAMUSHI (*natural size*).

or *semi*, so the *kutsuwamushi* is the most wonderful of night-crickets. It owes its name, which means "The Bridle-bit-Insect," to its noise, which resembles the jingling and ringing of the old-fashioned Japanese bridle-bit (*kutsuwa*). But the sound is really much louder and much more complicated than ever was the jingling of a single *kutsuwa;* and the accuracy of the comparison is not easily discerned while the creature is storming beside you.   Without the evidence of one's own eyes, it were hard to believe that so small a life could make so prodigious a noise.   Certainly the vibratory apparatus in this insect must be very complicated.   The sound begins with a thin sharp whizzing, as of leaking steam, and slowly strengthens; — then to the whizzing is suddenly added a quick dry clatter, as of castanets; — and then, as the whole machinery rushes into operation, you hear, high above the whizzing and the clatter, a torrent of rapid ringing tones like the tapping of a gong.   These, the last to begin, are also the first to cease;   then the castanets stop;   and finally the whizzing dies; — but the full orchestra may remain in operation for several hours at a time, without a pause.   Heard from far away at night the sound is pleasant, and is really so much like the ringing of a bridle-bit, that when you first listen to it you cannot but feel how much real poetry belongs to the name of this insect, — celebrated from of old as " playing at ghostly escort in ways where no man can pass."

The most ancient poem on the *kutsuwamushi*
is perhaps the following, by the Lady Idzumi-
Shikibu: —

> Waga seko wa
> Koma ni makasété
> Kinikeri to,
> Kiku ni kikasuru
> Kutsuwamushi kana !

— which might be thus freely rendered:

Listen ! — his bridle rings ; — that is surely my husband
Homeward hurrying now — fast as the horse can bear
      him ! . . .
Ah ! my ear was deceived ! — only the Kutsuwamushi !

KANTAN (*natural size*).

Kantan.

This insect — also called *kantan-gisu,* and *kantan-no-kirigirisu,* — is a dark-brown night-cricket. Its note — "*ʒi-ī-ī-i-in*" — is peculiar: I can only compare it to the prolonged twang of a bow-string. But this comparison is not satisfactory, because there is a penetrant metallic quality in the twang, impossible to describe.

VI

Besides poems about the chanting of particular insects, there are countless Japanese poems, ancient and modern, upon the voices of night-insects in general, — chiefly in relation to the autumn season. Out of a multitude I have selected and translated a few of the more famous only, as typical of the sentiment or fancy of hundreds. Although some of my renderings are far from literal as to language, I believe that they express with tolerable faithfulness the thought and feeling of the originals: —

Not for my sake alone, I know, is the autumn's coming; —
Yet, hearing the insects sing, at once my heart grows sad.
KOKINSHŪ.

Faint in the moonshine sounds the chorus of insect-voices:
To-night the sadness of autumn speaks in their plaintive
    tone.

I never can find repose in the chilly nights of autumn,
Because of the pain I hear in the insects' plaintive song.

How must it be in the fields where the dews a,e falling
    thickly!
In the insect-voices that reach me I hear the tingling of cold.

Never I dare to take my way through the grass in autumn:
Should I tread upon insect-voices[1] — what would my feel-
    ings be!

The song is ever the same, but the tones of the insects
    differ,
Maybe their sorrows vary, according to their hearts
                                IDZUMI-SHIKIBU.

Changed is my childhood's home — all but those insect-
    voices:
I think they are trying to speak of happier days that were.

These trembling dews on the grass — are they tears for the
    death of autumn? —
Tears of the insect-singers that now so sadly cry?

It might be thought that several of the poems
above given were intended to express either a real
or an affected sympathy with imagined insect-
pain. But this would be a wrong interpretation.

---

[1] *Mushi no koe fumu.*

In most compositions of this class, the artistic
purpose is to suggest, by indirect means, various
phases of the emotion of love, — especially that
melancholy which lends its own passional tone to
the aspects and the voices of nature.   The baroque
fancy that dew might be insect-tears, is by its
very exaggeration intended to indicate the extrav-
agance of grief, as well as to suggest that human
tears have been freshly shed.   The verses in which
a woman declares that her heart has become too
affectionate, since she cannot but feel for the bell-
insect during a heavy shower, really bespeak the
fond anxiety felt for some absent beloved, travelling in the time of the great rains.   Again, in the
lines about " treading on insect-voices," the dainty
scruple is uttered only as a hint of that intensification of feminine tenderness which love creates.
And a still more remarkable example of this indirect double-suggestiveness is offered by the little
poem prefacing this article, —

"O insect, insect ! — think you that Karma can be exhausted by song ?"

The Western reader would probably suppose that
the insect-condition, or insect-state-of-being, is
here referred to; but the real thought of the

speaker, presumably a woman, is that her own sorrow is the result of faults committed in former lives, and is therefore impossible to alleviate.

It will have been observed that a majority of the verses cited refer to autumn and to the sensations of autumn. Certainly Japanese poets have not been insensible to the real melancholy inspired by autumn, — that vague strange annual revival of ancestral pain: dim inherited sorrow of millions of memories associated through millions of years with the death of summer; — but in nearly every utterance of this melancholy, the veritable allusion is to grief of parting. With its color-changes, its leaf-whirlings, and the ghostly plaint of its insect-voïces, autumn Buddhistically symbolizes impermanency, the certainty of bereavement, the pain that clings to all desire, and the sadness of isolation.

But even if these poems on insects were primarily intended to shadow amorous emotion, do they not reflect also for us the subtlest influences of nature, — wild pure nature, — upon imagination and memory? Does not the place accorded to insect-melody, in the home-life as well as in the literature of Japan, prove an æsthetic sensibility developed in directions that yet remain for us almost unexplored? Does not the shrilling booth of the insect-seller at a night-festival proclaim even a popular and universal comprehension of things divined in the West only by our rarest poets : — the pleasure-pain of autumn's beauty, the weird sweetness of the voices of the night, the magical quickening of remembrance by echoes of forest and field? Surely we have something to learn from the people in whose mind the simple chant of a cricket can awaken whole fairy-swarms of tender and delicate fancies. We may boast of being their masters in the mechanical, — their teachers of the artificial in all its varieties of ugliness ; — but in the knowledge of the natural, — in the feeling of the joy and beauty of earth, — they exceed us like the Greeks of old. Yet perhaps it will be only when our blind aggressive industrialism has wasted and sterilized their paradise, — substituting everywhere for beauty the utilitarian, the conventional, the vulgar, the utterly hideous, — that we shall begin with remorseful amazement to comprehend the charm of that which we destroyed.

A Question in the Zen Texts

A Question in the Zen Texts

I

M Y friend opened a thin yellow volume of
that marvellous text which proclaims at
sight the patience of the Buddhist en-
graver. Movable Chinese types may be very
useful; but the best of which they are capable
is ugliness itself when compared with the beauty
of the old block-printing.

"I have a queer story for you," he said.

"A Japanese story?"

"No, — Chinese."

"What is the book?"

"According to Japanese pronunciation of the
Chinese characters of the title, we call it *Mu-
Mon-Kwan*, which means 'The Gateless Barrier.'
It is one of the books especially studied by the
Zen sect, or sect of Dhyâna. A peculiarity of
some of the Dhyâna texts, — this being a good
example, — is that they are not explanatory.

They only suggest. Questions are put; but the student must think out the answers for himself. He must *think* them out, but not write them. You know that Dhyana represents human effort to reach, through meditation, zones of thought beyond the range of verbal expression; and any thought once narrowed into utterance loses all Dhyana quality. . . . Well, this story is supposed to be true; but it is used only for a Dhyana question. There are three different Chinese versions of it; and I can give you the substance of the three."

Which he did as follows: —

II

—*The story of the girl Ts'ing, which is told in the Lui-shwo-li-hwan-ki, cited by the Ching-tang-luh, and commented upon in the Wu-mu-kwan (called by the Japanese Mu-Mon-Kwan), which is a book of the Zen sect* : —

There lived in Han-yang a man called Chang-Kien, whose child-daughter, Ts'ing, was of peerless beauty. He had also a nephew called Wang-Chau, — a very handsome boy. The

children played together, and were fond of each other. Once Kien jestingly said to his nephew:
— "Some day I will marry you to my little daughter." Both children remembered these words; and they believed themselves thus betrothed.

When Ts'ing grew up, a man of rank asked for her in marriage; and her father decided to comply with the demand. Ts'ing was greatly troubled by this decision. As for Chau, he was so much angered and grieved that he resolved to leave home, and go to another province. The next day he got a boat ready for his journey, and after sunset, without bidding farewell to any one, he proceeded up the river. But in the middle of the night he was startled by a voice calling to him, "Wait! — it is I!" — and he saw a girl running along the bank towards the boat. It was Ts'ing. Chau was unspeakably delighted. She sprang into the boat; and the lovers found their way safely to the province of Chuh.

In the province of Chuh they lived happily for six years; and they had two children. But Ts'ing could not forget her parents, and often longed to see them again. At last she said to her husband: — "Because in former time I could not bear to break the promise made to you, I ran away with you and forsook my parents, — although knowing that I owed them all possible duty and affection. Would it not now be well to try to obtain their forgiveness?" "Do not grieve yourself about that," said Chau; — "we shall go to see them." He ordered a boat to be prepared; and a few days later he returned with his wife to Han-yang.

According to custom in such cases, the husband first went to the house of Kien, leaving Ts'ing alone in the boat. Kien, welcomed his nephew with every sign of joy, and said: —

"How much I have been longing to see you! I was often afraid that something had happened to you."

Chau answered respectfully: —

"I am distressed by the undeserved kindness of your words. It is to beg your forgiveness that I have come."

But Kien did not seem to understand. He asked: —

"To what matter do you refer?"

"I feared," said Chau, "that you were angry with me for having run away with Ts'ing. I took her with me to the province of Chuh."

" What Ts'ing was that ? " asked Kien.

" Your daughter Ts'ing," answered Chau, beginning to suspect his father-in-law of some
malevolent design.

" What are you talking about ? " cried Kien,
with every appearance of astonishment. " My
daughter Ts'ing has been sick in bed all these
years, — ever since the time when you went
away."

" Your daughter Ts'ing," returned Chau, becoming angry, " has not been sick. She has
been my wife for six years ; and we have two
children ; and we have both returned to this
place only to seek your pardon. Therefore please
do not mock us ! "

For a moment the two looked at each other in
silence. Then Kien arose, and motioning to his
nephew to follow, led the way to an inner room
where a sick girl was lying. And Chau, to his
utter amazement, saw the face of Ts'ing, — beautiful, but strangely thin and pale.

" She cannot speak," explained the old man ;
" but she can understand." And Kien said to
her, laughingly : — " Chau tells me that you ran
away with him, and that you gave him two
children."

The sick girl looked at Chau, and smiled; but remained silent.

" Now come with me to the river," said the bewildered visitor to his father-in-law. " For I can assure you, — in spite of what I have seen in this house, — that your daughter Ts'ing is at this moment in my boat."

They went to the river; and there, indeed, was the young wife, waiting. And seeing her father, she bowed down before him, and besought his pardon.

Kien said to her : —

" If you really be my daughter, I have nothing but love for you. Yet though you seem to be my daughter, there is something which I cannot understand. . . . Come with us to the house."

So the three proceeded toward the house. As they neared it, they saw that the sick girl, — who had not before left her bed for years, — was coming to meet them, smiling as if much delighted. And the two Ts'ings approached each other. But then — nobody could ever tell how — they suddenly melted into each other, and became one body, one person, one Ts'ing, — even more beautiful than before, and showing no sign of sickness or of sorrow.

Kien said to Chau : —

"Ever since the day of your going, my daughter was dumb, and most of the time like a person who had taken too much wine. Now I know that her spirit was absent."

Ts'ing herself said : —

"Really I never knew that I was at home. I saw Chau going away in silent anger; and the same night I dreamed that I ran after his boat. . . . But now I cannot tell which was really I, — the I that went away in the boat, or the I that stayed at home."

III

"That is the whole of the story," my friend observed. "Now there is a note about it in the *Mu-Mon-Kwan* that may interest you. This note says : — 'The fifth patriarch of the Zen sect once asked a priest, — "*In the case of the separation of the spirit of the girl Ts'ing, which was the true Ts'ing?*"' It was only because of this question that the story was cited in the book. But the question is not answered. The author only remarks : — 'If you can decide which was the real Ts'ing, then you will have learned that to go out of one envelope and into another is merely like putting up at an inn. But if you have not yet reached this degree of enlightenment, take heed that you do not wander aimlessly about the world. Otherwise, when Earth, Water, Fire, and Wind shall suddenly be dissipated, you will be like a crab with seven hands and eight legs, thrown into boiling water. And in that time do not say that you were never told about the *Thing*.' . . . Now the *Thing* — "

" I do not want to hear about the Thing," I interrupted, — " nor about the crab with seven hands and eight legs. I want to hear about the clothes."

" What clothes ? "

" At the time of their meeting, the two Ts'ings would have been differently dressed, — very differently, perhaps ; for one was a maid, and the other a wife. Did the clothes of the two also blend together ? Suppose that one had a silk robe and the other a robe of cotton, would these have mixed into a texture of silk and cotton ? Suppose that one was wearing a blue girdle, and the other a yellow girdle, would the result have been a green girdle ? . . . Or did one Ts'ing simply slip out of her costume, and leave it on the ground, like the cast-off shell of a cicada?"

"None of the texts say anything about the clothes," my friend replied: "so I cannot tell you. But the subject is quite irrelevant, from the Buddhist point of view. The doctrinal question is the question of what I suppose you would call the personality of Ts'ing."

"And yet it is not answered," I said.

"It is best answered," my friend replied, "by not being answered."

"How so?"

"Because there is no such thing as personality."

The Literature of the Dead

The Literature of the Dead

Shindaréba koso ikitaré.

"Only because of having died, does one enter into life."
— *Buddhist proverb.*

I

BEHIND my dwelling, but hidden from view by a very lofty curtain of trees, there is a Buddhist temple, with a cemetery attached to it. The cemetery itself is in a grove of pines, many centuries old; and the temple stands in a great quaint lonesome garden. Its religious name is *Ji-shō-in;* but the people call it Kobudera, which means the Gnarled, or Knobby Temple, because it is built of undressed timber, — great logs of *hinoki*, selected for their beauty or strangeness of shape, and simply prepared for the builder by the removal of limbs and bark. But such gnarled and knobby wood is precious: it is of the hardest and most enduring, and costs far more than common building-material, — as might be divined from the fact that the beautiful alcoves and the choicest parts of Japanese interiors are finished with wood of a similar kind.   To build Kobudera was an undertaking worthy of a prince; and, as a matter of history, it was a prince who erected it, for a place of family worship.   There is a doubtful tradition that two designs were submitted to him by the architect, and that he chose the more fantastic one under the innocent impression that undressed timber would prove cheap.   But whether it owes its existence to a mistake or not, Kobudera remains one of the most interesting temples of Japan.   The public have now almost forgotten its existence; — but it was famous in the time of Iyemitsu; and its appellation, Ji-shō-in, was taken from the kaimyō of one of the great Shogun's ladies, whose superb tomb may be seen in its cemetery.   Before Meiji, the temple was isolated among woods and fields; but the city has now swallowed up most of the green spaces that once secluded it, and has pushed out the ugliest of new streets directly in front of its gate.

This gate — a structure of gnarled logs, with a tiled and tilted Chinese roof — is a fitting pref-

GATE OF KOBUDERA

ace to the queer style of the temple itself. From
either gable-end of the gate-roof, a demon-head,
grinning under triple horns, looks down upon the
visitor.[1] Within, except at the hours of prayer,
all is green silence. Children do not play in the

[1] Such figures are really elaborate tiles, and are called
onigawara, or "demon-tiles." It may naturally be asked
why demon-heads should be ever placed above Buddhist
gate-ways. Originally they were not intended to represent
demons, in the Buddhist sense, but guardian-spirits whose
duty it was to drive demons away. The *onigawara* were
introduced into Japan either from China or Korea — not
improbably Korea; for we read that the first roof-tiles
made in Japan were manufactured shortly after the intro-
duction of the new faith by Korean priests, and under the
supervision of Shōtoku Taishi, the princely founder and
supporter of Japanese Buddhism. They were baked at
Koizumi-mura, in Yamato; — but we are not told whether
there were any of this extraordinary shape among them.
It is worth while remarking that in Korea to-day you can
see hideous faces painted upon house-doors, — even upon
the gates of the royal palace; and these, intended merely
to frighten away evil spirits, suggest the real origin of the
demon-tiles. The Japanese, on first seeing such tiles, called
them demon-tiles because the faces upon them resembled
those conventionally given to Buddhist demons; and now
that their history has been forgotten, they are popularly
supposed to represent demon-guardians. There would be
nothing contrary to Buddhist faith in the fancy; — for
there are many legends of good demons. Besides, in the
eternal order of divine law, even the worst demon must at
last become a Buddha.

7

court — perhaps because the temple is a private
one. The ground is everywhere hidden by a fine
thick moss of so warm a color, that the brightest
foliage of the varied shrubbery above it looks
sombre by contrast; and the bases of walls, the
pedestals of monuments, the stonework of the
bell-tower, the masonry of the ancient well, are
muffled with the same luminous growth. Maples
and pines and cryptomerias screen the façade of
the temple; and, if your visit be in autumn, you
may find the whole court filled with the sweet
heavy perfume of the *mokusei*[1]-blossom. After
having looked at the strange temple, you would
find it worth while to enter the cemetery, by the
black gate on the west side of the court.

I like to wander in that cemetery, — partly because in the twilight of its great trees, and in the
silence of centuries which has gathered about
them, one can forget the city and its turmoil, and
dream out of space and time, — but much more
because it is full of beauty, and of the poetry of
great faith. Indeed of such poetry it possesses
riches quite exceptional. Each Buddhist sect has

[1] *Osmanthus fragrans.* This is one of the very few
Japanese plants having richly-perfumed flowers.

its own tenets, rites, and forms; and the special character of these is reflected in the iconography and epigraphy of its burial-grounds, — so that for any experienced eye a Tendai graveyard is readily distinguishable from a Shingon graveyard, or a Zen graveyard from one belonging to a Nichiren congregation. But at Kobudera the inscriptions and the sculptures peculiar to several Buddhist sects can be studied side by side. Founded for the Hokké, or Nichiren rite, the temple nevertheless passed, in the course of generations, under the control of other sects — the last being the Tendai; — and thus its cemetery now offers a most interesting medley of the emblems and the epitaphic formularies of various persuasions. It was here that I first learned, under the patient teaching of an Oriental friend, something about the Buddhist literature of the dead.

No one able to feel beauty could refuse to confess the charm of the old Buddhist cemeteries, — with their immemorial trees, their evergreen mazes of shrubbery trimmed into quaintest shapes, the carpet-softness of their mossed paths, the weird but unquestionable art of their monuments. And no great knowledge of Buddhism is

needed to enable you, even at first sight, to understand something of this art. You would recognize the lotos chiselled upon tombs or water-tanks,
and would doubtless observe that the designs of
the pedestals represent a lotos of eight petals, —
though you might not know that these eight
petals symbolize the Eight Intelligences. You
would recognize the *manji*, or svastika, figuring
the Wheel of the Law, — though ignorant of
its relation to the Mahâyâna philosophy. You
would perhaps be able to recognize also the
images of certain Buddhas, — though not aware
of the meaning of their attitudes or emblems in
relation to mystical ecstasy or to the manifestation of the Six Supernatural Powers. And you
would be touched by the simple pathos of the
offerings, — the incense and the flowers before
the tombs, the water poured out for the dead, —
even though unable to divine the deeper pathos
of the beliefs that make the cult. But unless an
excellent Chinese scholar as well as a Buddhist
philosopher, all book-knowledge of the great
religion would still leave you helpless in a world
of riddles. The marvellous texts, — the exquisite Chinese scriptures chiselled into the granite
of tombs, or limned by a master-brush upon the

smooth wood of the *sotoba*, — will yield their secrets only to an interpreter of no common powers. And the more you become familiar with their aspect, the more the mystery of them tantalizes, — especially after you have learned that a literal translation of them would mean, in the majority of cases, exactly nothing!

What strange thoughts have been thus recorded and yet concealed? Are they complex and subtle as the characters that stand for them? Are they beautiful also like those characters, — with some undreamed-of, surprising beauty, such as might inform the language of another planet?

II

As for subtlety and complexity, much of this mortuary literature is comparable to the Veil of Isis. Behind the mystery of the text — in which almost every character has two readings — there is the mystery of the phrase ; and again behind this are successions of riddles belonging to a gnosticism older than all the wisdom of the Occident, and deep as the abysses of Space. Fortunately the most occult texts are also the least interesting, and bear little relation to the purpose of this essay. The majority are attached, not to the sculptured, but to the written and impermanent literature of cemeteries, — not to the stone monuments, but to the sotoba: those tall narrow laths of unpainted wood which are planted above the graves at fixed, but gradually increasing intervals, during a period of one hundred years.[1]

The uselessness of any exact translation of these inscriptions may be exemplified by a word-for-word rendering of two sentences written upon the sotoba used by the older sects. What meaning can you find in such a term as "Law-sphere-substance-nature-wisdom," or such an invocation as "Ether, Wind, Fire, Water, Earth!" — for an invocation it really is? To understand these

---

[1] The word "sotoba" is identical with the Sanscrit "stûpa." Originally a mausoleum, and later a simple monument — commemorative or otherwise, — the stûpa was introduced with Buddhism into China, and thence, perhaps by way of Korea, into Japan. Chinese forms of the stone stûpa are to be found in many of the old Japanese temple-grounds. The wooden *sotoba* is only a symbol of the stûpa; and the more elaborate forms of it plainly suggest its history. The slight carving along its upper edges represents that superimposition of cube, sphere, crescent, pyramid, and body-pyriform (symbolizing the Five Great Elements), which forms the design of the most beautiful funeral monuments.

SOTOBA IN KOBUDERA CEMETERY

(*The upper characters are "BONTI"—modified Sanskrit*)

words one must first know that, in the doctrine
of the mystical sects, the universe is composed
of Five Great Elements which are identical with
Five Buddhas; that each of the Five Buddhas
contains the rest; and that the Five are One by
essence, though varying in their phenomenal man-
ifestations. The name of an element has thus
three significations. The word Fire, for example,
means flame as objective appearance; it means
flame also as the manifestation of a particular
Buddha; and it likewise means the special quality
of wisdom or power attributed to that Buddha.
Perhaps this doctrine will be more easily understood by the help of the following Shingon clas-
sification of the Five Elements in their Buddhist
relations: —

I. *Hō-kai-tai-shō-chi*

(Sansc. Dhârma-dhâtu-prakrit-gñâna), or "Law-sphere-
substance-nature-wisdom," — signifying the wisdom that
becomes the substance of things. This is the element Ether.
Ether personified is Dai-Nichi-Nyōrai, the "Great Sun-Bud-
dha" (Mahâvairokana Tathâgata), who "holds the seal of
Wisdom."

II. *Dai-en-kyō-chi*

(Âdarsana-gñâna), or "Great-round-mirror-wisdom," —
that is to say the divine power making images manifest.
This is the element Earth. Earth personified is Ashuku
Nyōrai, the "Immovable Tathâgata" (Akshobhya).

III.   *Byō-dō-shō-chi*

(Samatâ-gñâna), " Even-equal-nature-wisdom," — that is, the wisdom making no distinction of persons or of things. The element Fire. Personified, Fire is Hō-shō Nyōrai, or "Gem-Birth" Buddha (Ratnasambhava Tathâgata), presiding over virtue and happiness.

IV.   *Myō-kwan-ӡatsu-chi*

(Pratyavekshana-gñâna),   "Wondrously-observing-considering-wisdom;" — that is, the wisdom distinguishing clearly truth from error, destroying doubts, and presiding over the preaching of the Law. The element Water. Water personified is Amida Nyōrai, the Buddha of Immeasurable Light (Amitâbha Tathâgata).

V.   *Jō-shō-sa-chi*

(Krityânushthâna-gñâna), the " Wisdom-of-accomplishing-what-is-to-be-done; " — that is to say, the divine wisdom that helps beings to reach Nirvana. The element Air. Air personified is Fu-kū-jō-ju, the "Unfailing-of-Accomplishment," — more commonly called Fuku-Nyōrai (Amoghasiddhi, or Sâkyamuni).[1]

Now the doctrine that each of the Five Buddhas contains the rest, and that all are essentially One,

[1] These relations of the elements to the Buddhas named are not, however, permanently fixed in the doctrine, — for obvious philosophical reasons. Sometimes Sakyamuni is identified with Ether, and Amitâbha with Air, etc., etc. In the above enumeration I have followed the order taken by Professor Bunyiu Nanjio, who nevertheless suggests that this order is not to be considered perpetual.

is symbolized in these texts by an extraordinary use of characters called *Bon-ji,* — which are recognizably Sanscrit letters. The name of each element can be written with any one of four characters, — all having for Buddhists the same meaning, though differing as to sound and form. Thus the characters standing for Fire would read, according to Japanese pronunciation, *Ra*, *Ran*, *Raän*, and *Raku ;* — and the characters signifying Ether, *Kya*, *Ken*, *Keën*, and *Kyaku*. By different combinations of the twenty characters making the five sets, different supernatural powers and different Buddhas are indicated ; and the indication is further helped by an additional symbolic character, called *Shū-ji* or " seed-word," placed immediately after the names of the elements. The reader will now comprehend the meaning of the invocatory " Ether, Wind, Fire, Water, Earth ! " and of the strange names of divine wisdom written upon sotoba ; but the enigmas offered by even a single sotoba may be much more complicated than the foregoing examples suggest. There are unimaginable acrostics ; there are rules, varying according to sect, for the position of texts in relation to the points of the compass ; and there are kabalisms

based upon the multiple values of certain Chinese
ideographs. The whole subject of esoteric inscriptions would require volumes to explain; and the
reader will not be sorry, I fancy, to abandon it at
this point in favor of texts possessing a simpler
and a more humane interest.

The really attractive part of Buddhist cemetery-
literature mostly consists of sentences taken from
the sûtras or the sastras; and the attraction is
due not only to the intrinsic beauty of the faith
which these sentences express, but also to the
fact that they will be found to represent, in
epitome, a complete body of Buddhist doctrine.
Like the mystical inscriptions above-mentioned,
they belong to the sotoba, not to the grave-
stones; but, while the invocations usually occupy
the upper and front part of the sotoba, these
sutra-texts are commonly written upon the back.
In addition to scriptural and invocatory texts,
each sotoba bears the name of the giver, the
kaimyō of the dead, and the name of a commemorative anniversary. Sometimes a brief
prayer is also inscribed, or a statement of the
pious purpose inspiring the erection of the sotoba.
Before considering the scripture-texts proper, in
relation to their embodiment of doctrine, I sub-

mit examples of the general character and plan of
sotoba inscriptions.   They are written upon both
sides of the wood, be it observed ; but I have not
thought it necessary to specify which texts belong
to the front, and which to the back of the sotoba,
— since the rules concerning such position differ
according to sect : —

I. — SOTOBA OF THE NICHIREN SECT.

(Invocation.)

*Ether, Wind, Fire, Water, Earth! — Hail
to the Sutra of the Lotos of the Good Law!*

(Commemorative text.)

To-day, the service of the third year has been performed
in order that our lay-brother [*kaimyō*] may be enabled to
cut off the bonds of illusion, to open the Eye of Enlightenment, to remain free from all pain, and to enter into bliss.

(Sastra text.)

MYŌ-HŌ-KYŌ-RIKI-SOKU-SHIN-JŌ-BUTSU !

Even this body [of flesh] by the virtue of the Sutra of
the Excellent Law, enters into Buddhahood.

II. — SOTOBA OF THE NICHIREN SECT.

(Invocation.)

*Hail to the Sutra of the Lotos of the Good
Law!*

(Commemorative text.)

The rite of feeding the hungry spirits having been ful-
filled, and the service for the dead having been performed,
this sotoba is set up in commemoration of the service and
the offerings made with prayer for the salvation of Buddha
on behalf of — (*kaimyō* follows).

(Prayer — with English translation.)

> *Gan i shi kudoku*
> *Fu-gyū o issai*
> *Gatō yo shujō*
> *Kai-gu jō butsudo.*

By virtue of this good action I beseech that the merit of
it may be extended to all, and that we and all living beings
may fulfil the Way of Buddha.[1]

*The fifth day of the seventh month of the
thirtieth year of Meiji, by —— ——, this sotoba
has been set up.*

III. — SOTOBA OF THE JŌDO SECT.

(Invocation.)

Hail to the Buddha Amida !

(Commemorative mention.)

This for the sake of — (*here kaimyō* follows).

---

[1] The above prayer is customarily said after having read
a sûtra, or copied a sacred text, or caused a Buddhist service to be performed.

(Sutra text.)

The Buddha of the Golden Mouth, who possesses the Great-Round-Mirror-Wisdom,[1] has said : " The glorious light of Amida illuminates all the worlds of the Ten Directions, and takes into itself and never abandons all living beings who fix their thoughts upon that Buddha!"

IV. — SOTOBA OF THE ZEN SECT.

(Sastra text.)

The Dai-en-kyō-chi-kyō declares : — " By entering deeply into meditation, one may behold the Buddhas of the Ten Directions."

(Commemorative text.)

That the noble Elder Sister[2] Chi-Shō-In-Kō-Un-Tei-Myō,[3] now dwelling in the House of Shining Wisdom, may instantly attain to Bodhi.[4]

---

[1] Dai-en-kyō-chi (Âdarsana-gñâna). Amida is the Japanese form of the name Amitâbha.

[2] " Great (or Noble) Elder Sister " is the meaning of the title *dai-shi* affixed to the *kaimyō* of a woman. In the rite of the Zen sect *dai-shi* always signifies a married woman; *shin-nyo*, a maid.

[3] This *kaimyō*, or posthumous name, literally signifies: Radiant-Chastity-Beaming-Through-Luminous-Clouds.

[4] The Supreme Wisdom; the state of Buddhahood.

(Prayer.)

Let whomsoever looks upon this sotoba be forever delivered from the Three Evil Ways.[1]

(Record.)

In the thirtieth year of Meiji, on the first day of the fifth month, by the house of Inouyé, this sotoba has been set up.

The foregoing will doubtless suffice as specimens of the ordinary forms of inscription. The Buddha praised or invoked is always the Buddha especially revered by the sect from whose sutra or sastra the quotation is chosen; — sometimes also the divine power of a Bodhisattva is extolled, as in the following Zen inscription : —

" The Sutra of Kwannon says : — ' In all the provinces of all the countries in the Ten Directions, there is not even one temple where Kwannon is not self-revealed.' "

Sometimes the scripture text more definitely assumes the character of a praise-offering, as the following juxtaposition suggests : —

[1] *San-Akudō*, — the three unhappy conditions of Hell, of the World of Hungry Spirits (*Pretas*), and of Animal Existence.

" *The Buddha of Immeasurable Light illuminates all worlds in the Ten Directions of
Space.*"

This for the sake of the swift salvation into Buddhahood
of our lay-brother named the Great-Secure-Retired-Scholar.

Sometimes we also find a verse of praise or an
invocation addressed to the apotheosized spirit of
the founder of the sect, — a common example
being furnished by the sotoba of the Shingon
rite : —

" *Hail to the Great Teacher Haijō-Kongō!* " [1]

Rarely the little prayer for the salvation of the
dead assumes, as in the following beautiful example, the language of unconscious poetry : —

" *This for the sake of our noble Elder Sister
——. May the Lotos of Bliss by virtue of these
prayers be made to bloom for her, and to bear
the fruit of Buddhahood!* " [2]

But usually the prayers are of the simplest, and
differ from each other only in the use of peculiar
Buddhist terms : —

[1] " Haijō Kongō " means "the Diamond of Universal
Enlightenment : " it is the honorific appellation of Kūkai
or Kobodaishi, founder of the Shingon-Shū.

[2] From a Zen sotoba.

— " This for the sake of the true happiness of our lay-brother — [*kaimyō*], — that he may obtain the Supreme Perfect Enlightenment."

— " This tower is set up for the sake of ——, that he may obtain complete Sambodhi." [1]

— " This precious tower and these offerings for the sake of —— ——, — that he may obtain the *Anattra-Sammyak-Sambodhi*." [2]

One other subject of interest belonging to the merely commemorative texts of sotoba remains to be mentioned, — the names of certain Buddhist services for the dead.   There are two classes of such services: those performed within one hundred days after death, and those celebrated at fixed intervals during a term of one hundred years, — on the 1st, 2d, 7th, 13th, 17th, 24th, 33d, 50th, and 100th anniversaries of the death.   In the Zen rite these commemorative services — (perhaps we might call them masses) — have singular mystical names by which they are recorded upon the sotoba of the sect, — such

---

[1] In Japanese " Sanbodai."   The term " tower " refers of course to the *sotoba*, the symbol of a real tower, or at least of the desire to erect such a monument, were it possible.

[2] In Japanese, *Anuka-tara-sanmaku-sanbodai*, — the supreme form of Buddhist enlightenment.

as Lesser Happiness, Greater Happiness, Broad Repose, The Bright Caress, and The Great Caress.

But we shall now turn to the study of the scripture-texts proper, — those citations from sûtra or sastra which form the main portion of a sotoba-writing ; expounding the highest truth of Buddhist belief, or speaking the deepest thought of Eastern philosophy.

III

At the beginning of my studies in the Kobudera cemetery, I was not less impressed by the quiet cheerfulness of the sotoba-texts, than by their poetry and their philosophy. In none did I find even a shadow of sadness : the greater number were utterances of a faith that seemed to me wider and deeper than our own, — sublime proclamations of the eternal and infinite nature of Thought, the unity of all mind, and the certainty of universal salvation. And other surprises awaited me in this strange literature. Texts or fragments of texts, that at first rendering appeared of the simplest, would yield to learned commentary profundities of significance absolutely startling. Phrases, seemingly artless, would suddenly reveal a dual suggestiveness, — a two-fold idealism, — a beauty at once exoteric and mystical. Of this latter variety of inscription the following is a good example: —

" The flower having bloomed last night, the World has become fragrant." [1]

In the language of the higher Buddhism, this means that through death a spirit has been released from the darkness of illusion, even as the perfume of a blossom is set free at the breaking of the bud, and that the divine Absolute, or World of Law, is refreshed by the new presence, as a whole garden might be made fragrant by the blooming of some precious growth. But in the popular language of Buddhism, the same words signify that in the Lotos-Lake of Paradise another magical flower has opened for the Apparitional Rebirth into highest bliss of the being loved and lost on earth, and that Heaven rejoices for the advent of another Buddha.

But I desire rather to represent the general result of my studies, than to point out the special

[1] From a sotoba of the Jodo sect.

beauties of this epitaphic literature : and my purpose will be most easily attained by arranging
and considering the inscriptions in a certain
doctrinal order.

A great variety of sotoba-texts refer, directly
or indirectly, to the Lotos-Flower Paradise of
Amida, — or, as it is more often called, the Paradise of the West.   The following are typical : —

*" The Amida-Kyō says : — ' All who enter into
that country enter likewise into that state of
virtue from which there can be no turning
back.' "* [1]

*" The Text of Gold proclaims : — ' In that
world they receive bliss only : therefore that
world is called Gokuraku, — exceeding bliss.' "* [2]

---

[1] From a sotoba of the Jōdo sect. The Amida-Kyō, or
Sûtra of Amida, is the Japanese [Chinese] version of the
smaller Sukhâvatî-Vyûha Sûtra.

[2] *Gokuraku* is the common word in Japan for the Buddhist heaven.   The above inscription, translated for me from
a sotoba of the Jōdo sect, is an abbreviated form of a verse
in the Smaller Sukhâvatî-Vyûha (see *Buddhist Mahâyâna
Texts :* " Sacred Books of the East "), which Max Müller has
thus rendered in full : — " In that world Sukhâvatî, O Sâri-
putra, there is neither bodily nor mental pain for living
beings.   The sources of happiness are innumerable there.
For that reason is that world called Sukhâvatî, the happy."

" Hail unto the Lord Amida Buddha! The
Golden Mouth has said, — ' All living beings that
fix their thoughts upon the Buddha shall be re-
ceived and welcomed into his Paradise; — never
shall they be forsaken.'" [1]

But texts like these, though dear to popular
faith, make no appeal to the higher Buddhism,
which admits heaven as a temporary condition
only, not to be desired by the wise. Indeed, the
Mahâyâna texts, describing Sukhâvatî, themselves
suggest its essentially illusive character, — a world
of jewel-lakes and perfumed airs and magical
birds, but a world also in which the voices of
winds and waters and singers perpetually preach
the unreality of self and the impermanency of all
things. And even the existence of this Western
Paradise might seem to be denied in other sotoba-
texts of deeper significance, — such as this : —

" Originally there is no East or West : where
then can South or North be?" [2]

" Originally," — that is to say, in relation to the
Infinite. The relations and the ideas of the Con-
ditioned cease to exist for the Unconditioned. Yet

[1] From a sotoba of the Jōdo sect.
[2] Sotoba of the Jōdo sect.

this truth does not really imply denial of other worlds of relation,—states of bliss to which the strong may rise, and states of pain to which the weak may descend.   It is a reminder only.   All conditions are impermanent, and so, in the profounder sense, unreal.   The Absolute,—the Supreme Buddha,—is the sole Reality.   This doctrine appears in many sotoba-inscriptions:—

" The Blue Mountain of itself remains eternally unmoved: the White Clouds come of themselves and go." [1]

By "the Blue Mountain" is meant the Sole Reality of Mind;—by "the White Clouds," the phenomenal universe.   Yet the universe exists but as a dream of Mind:—

" If any one desire to obtain full knowledge of all the Buddhas of the past, the present, and the future, let him learn to comprehend the true nature of the World of Law.   Then will he perceive that all things are but the production of Mind." [2]

" By the learning and the practice of the True

---

[1] Sotoba of the Jōdo sect.
[2] Sotoba of the Zen sect.

Doctrine, the Non-Apparent becomes [for us]
the only Reality." [1]

The universe is a phantom, and a phantom
likewise the body of man, together with all emotions, ideas, and memories that make up the
complex of his sensuous Self.   But is this evanes-
cent Self the whole of man's inner being?   Not
so, proclaim the sotoba : —

" All living beings have the nature of Buddha.
The Nyōrai,[2] *eternally living, is alone un-*
changeable." [3]

" The Kegon-Kyō [4] *declares : — ' In all living*
creatures there exists, and has existed from the
beginning, the Real-Law Nature : all by their
nature contain the original essence of Buddha.' "

Sharing the nature of the Unchangeable, we
share the Eternal Reality.   In the highest sense,
man also is divine : —

" The Mind becomes Buddha : the Mind itself
is Buddha." [5]

[1] Sotoba of the Zen sect.   [2] Tathâgata.

[3] From a sotoba of the Zen sect.

[4] Avatamsaka Sûtra. — This text is also from a Zen
sotoba.

[5] From a tombstone of the Jōdo sect.   The text is evidently from the Chinese version of the Amitâyur-Dhy-

"In the Engaku-Kyō[1] it is written: 'Now for the first time I perceive that all living beings have the original Buddha-nature, — wherefore Birth and Death and Nirvana have become for me as a dream of the night that is gone.'"

Yet what of the Buddhas who successively melt into Nirvana, and nevertheless "return in their order"? Are they, too, phantoms? — is their individuality also unreal? Probably the question admits of many different answers, — since there is a Buddhist Realism as well as a Buddhist Idealism; but, for present purposes, the following famous text is a sufficient reply : —

NAMU ITSU SHIN SAN-ZÉ SHŌ BUTSU!

"Hail to all the Buddhas of the Three Existences,[2] who are but one in the One Mind!" [3]

âna-Sûtra (see *Buddhist Mahâyâna Texts:* "Sacred Books of the East"). It reads in the English version thus: — "In fine, it is your mind that becomes Buddha; — nay, it is your mind that is indeed Buddha."

[1] Pratyeka-Buddha sastra? — From a sotoba of the Zen sect.

[2] *San-zé,* or *mitsu-yo,* — the Past, Present, and Future.

[3] "Mind" is here expressed by the character *shin* or *kokoro.* — The text is from a Zen sotoba, but is used also, I am told, by the mystical sects of Tendai and Shingon.

In relation to the Absolute, no difference exists even between gods and men : —

" *The Golden Verse of the Jō-sho-sa-chi* [1] *says :* — '*This doctrine is equal and alike for all; there is neither superior nor inferior, neither above nor below.'* "

Nay, according to a still more celebrated text, there is not even any difference of personality : —

JI TA HŌ KAI BYŌ DŌ RI YAKU.

" *The ' I ' and the ' Not-I ' are not different in the World of Law : both are favored alike."* [2]

And a still more wonderful text — (to my thinking, the most remarkable of all Buddhist texts) — declares that the world itself, phantom though it be, is yet not different from Mind : —

SŌ MOKU KOKU DŌ SHITSU KAI JŌ BUTSU.

" *Grass, trees, countries, the earth itself, — all these shall enter wholly into Buddhahood."* [3]

---

[1] Krityânushthâna-gñâna. — The text is from a sotoba of the Shingon sect.

[2] More literally, " Self and Other : " i. e., the Ego and the Non-Ego in the meaning of " I " and " Thou." There is no " I " and " Thou " in Buddhahood. — This text was copied from a Zen sotoba.

[3] From a Zen sotoba.

Literally, "shall become Buddha;" that is, they shall enter into Buddhahood or Nirvana. All that we term matter will be transmuted therefore into Mind, — Mind with the attributes of Infinite Sentiency, Infinite Vision, and Infinite Knowledge. As phenomenon, matter is unreal; but transcendentally it belongs by its ultimate nature to the Sole Reality.

Such a philosophical position is likely to puzzle the average reader. To call matter and mind but two aspects of the Ultimate Reality will not seem irrational to students of Herbert Spencer. But to say that matter is a phenomenon, an illusion, a dream, explains nothing; — as phenomenon it exists, and having a destiny attributed to it, must be considered objectively. Equally unsatisfying is the statement that phenomena are aggregates of Karma. What is the nature of the particles of the aggregate? Or, in plainest language, what is the illusion made of?

Not in the original Buddhist scriptures, and still less in the literature of Buddhist cemeteries, need the reply be sought. Such questions are dealt with in the sastras rather than in the sûtras; — also in various Japanese commentaries upon both. A friend has furnished me with some

very curious and unfamiliar Shingon texts containing answers to the enigma.

The Shingon sect, 1 may observe, is a mystical
sect, which especially proclaims the identity of
mind and substance, and boldly carries out the
doctrine to its furthest logical consequences. Its
founder and father Kū-kai, better known as Kōbōdaishi, declared in his book *Hizōki* that matter is
not different in essence from spirit. " As to the
doctrine of grass, trees, and things non-sentient
becoming Buddhas " he writes, " I say that the
refined forms [*ultimate nature*] of spiritual bodies
consist of the Five Great Elements; that Ether [1]
consists of the Five Great Elements ; and that
the refined forms of bodies spiritual, of ether, of
plants, of trees, consequently pervade all space.
This ether, these plants and trees, are themselves
spiritual bodies. To the eye of flesh, plants and
trees appear to be gross matter. But to the eye

[1] The Chinese word literally means " void," — as in the
expression " Void Supreme," to signify the state of Nirvana.
But the philosophical reference here is to the ultimate substance, or primary matter ; and the rendering of the term
by " Ether " (rather in the Greek than the modern sense,
of course) has the sanction of Bunyiu Nanjio, and the approval of other eminent Sanscrit and Chinese scholars.

of the Buddha *they are composed of minute spiritual entities.*   Therefore, even without any change in their substance, there can be no error or impropriety in our calling them Buddhas."

The use of the term "non-sentient" in the foregoing would seem to involve a contradiction; but this is explained away by a dialogue in the book *Shi-man-gi* : —

Q. — Are not grass and trees sometimes called sentient?
A. — They can be so called.
Q. — But they have also been called non-sentient: how can they be called sentient?
A. — In all substance from the beginning exists the impress of the wisdom-nature of the Nyōrai (*Tathâgata*): therefore to call such things sentient is not error.

"Potentially sentient," the reader might conclude; but this conclusion would be wrong.   The Shingon thought is not of a potential sentiency, but of a latent sentiency which although to us non-apparent and non-imaginable, is nevertheless both real and actual.   Commenting upon the words of Kōbōdaishi above cited, the great priest Yū-kai not only reiterates the opinion of his master, but asserts that it is absurd to deny that plants, trees, and what we call inaminate objects, can practise virtue !   "Since Mind," he declares,

" pervades the whole World of Law, the grasses, plants, trees, and earth pervaded by it must all have mind, and must turn their mind to Buddha-hood and practise virtue. Do not doubt the doctrine of our sect, regarding the Non-Duality of the Pervading and the Pervaded, merely because of the distinction made in common parlance between Matter and Mind." As for *how* plants or stones can practise virtue, the sûtras indeed have nothing to say. But that is because the sûtras, being intended for man, teach only what man should know and do.

The reader will now, perhaps, be better able to follow out the really startling Buddhist hypothesis of the nature of matter to its more than startling conclusion. (It must not be contemned because of the fantasy of five elements ; for these are declared to be only modes of one ultimate.) All forms of what we call matter are really but aggregates of spiritual units ; and all apparent differences of substance represent only differences of combination among these units. The differences of combination are caused by special tendencies and affinities of the units ; — the tendency of each being the necessary result of its particular evolutional history — (using the term " evolu-

tional " in a purely ethical sense). All integra-
tions of apparent substance, — the million suns
and planets of the universe, — represent only the
affinities of such ghostly ultimates ; and every
human act or thought registers itself through
enormous time by some knitting or loosening of
forces working for good or evil.

Grass, trees, earth, and all things seem to us
what they are not, simply because the eye of
flesh is blind. Life itself is a curtain hiding
reality, — somewhat as the vast veil of day con-
ceals from our sight the countless orbs of Space.
But the texts of the cemeteries proclaim that the
purified mind, even while prisoned within the
body, may enter for moments of ecstasy into
union with the Supreme : —

*" The One Bright Moon illuminates the mind
in the meditation called Zenjō."* [1]

The " One Bright Moon " is the Supreme
Buddha. By the pure of heart He may even be
seen : —

[1] Literally, "illuminates the Zenjō-mind." Zenjō is the
Sanscrit *Dhyâna*. It is believed that in real *Dhyâna* the
mind can hold communication with the Absolute. — From
a sotoba of the Zen sect.

" Hail unto the Wondrous Law! By attaining to the state of single-mindedness we behold the Buddha." [1]

Greater delight there is none : —

" Incomparable the face of the Nyōrai, — surpassing all beauty in this world!" [2]

But to see the face of one Buddha is to see all : —

" The Dai-en-kyō-chi-kyō [3] *says : — ' By entering deeply into the meditation Zenjō, one may see all the Buddhas of the Ten Directions of Space.'"*

" The Golden Mouth has said : — ' He whose mind can discern the being of one Buddha, may easily behold three, four, five Buddhas, — nay, all the Buddhas of the Three Existences.'" [4]

Which mystery is thus explained : —

---

[1] From a sotoba of the Tendai sect.
[2] From a Jōdo sotoba.
[3] Literally, "the Great-Round-Mirror-Wisdom-Sûtra." Sansc., *Adarsana-gñâna.* — From a Zen sotoba.
[4] Sotoba of the Zen sect.

*" The Myō-kwan-satsu-chi-kyō [1] has said : —
The mind that detaches itself from all things
becomes the very mind of Buddha."* [2]

Visitors to the older Buddhist temples of Japan
can scarcely fail to notice the remarkable character of the gilded aureoles attached to certain
images.   These aureoles, representing circles,
disks, or ovals of glory, contain numbers of little
niches shaped like archings or whirls of fire, each
enshrining a Buddha or a Bodhisattva.   A verse
of the Amitâyur-Dhyâna Sûtra might have suggested this symbolism to the Japanese sculptors :
—*" In the halo of that Buddha there are Buddhas innumerable as the sands of the Ganga."* [3]
Icon and verse alike express that doctrine of the
One in Many suggested by the foregoing sotoba-
texts ; and the assurance that he who sees one
Buddha can see all, may further be accepted as
signifying that he who perceives one great truth
fully, will be able to perceive countless truths.

But even to the spiritually blind the light must
come at last.   A host of cemetery texts proclaim

---

[1] *Pratyavekshana-gñâna.*

[2] From a Zen sotoba.

[3] *Buddhist Mahâyâna Texts :* "Sacred Books of the
East," vol. xlix. p. 180.

the Infinite Love that watches all, and the certainty of ultimate and universal salvation : —

" Possessing all the Virtues and all the Powers, the Eyes of the Infinite Compassion behold all living creatures." [1]

" The Kongō-takara-tō-mei [2] proclaims : — ' All living beings in the Six States of Existence [3] shall be delivered from the bonds of attachment ; their minds and their bodies alike shall be freed from desire ; and they shall obtain the Supreme Enlightenment.' "

" The Sûtra says : — ' Changing the hearts of all beings, I cause them to enter upon the Way of Buddhahood.' " [4]

Yet the supreme conquest can be achieved only by self-effort : —

" Through the destruction of the Three Poisons [5]

---

[1] From a sotoba of the Zen sect.

[2] Lit.: "the Inscription of the Tower of Diamond," — name of a Buddhist text.

[3] The Six States of Existence are Heaven, Man, Demons, Hell, Hungry Spirits (*Pretas*), and Animals. — The above is from a Zen sotoba.

[4] Sotoba of the Nichiren sect.

[5] *San-doku* or *Mitsu-no-doku*, viz.: — **Anger, Ignorance,** and Desire. — From a Zen sotoba.

one may rise above the Three States of Existence."

The Three Existences signify time past, present, and future.   To rise above — (more literally, to "emerge from") — the Three Existences means therefore to pass beyond Space and Time, — to become one with the Infinite.   The conquest of Time is indeed possible only for a Buddha ; but all shall become Buddhas.   Even a woman, while yet a woman, may reach Buddhahood, as this Nichiren text bears witness, inscribed above the grave of a girl : —

KAI YO KEN PI RYŌ-NYŌ JŌ BUTSU.

" All beheld from afar the Dragon Maiden become a Buddha."

The reference is to the beautiful legend of Sâgara, the daughter of the Nâga-king, in the *Myō-hō-rengé-kyō.*[1]

[1] Japanese title of the Saddhârma-Pundarika Sûtra. See, for legend, chap. xi. of Kern's translation in the *Sacred Books of the East* series.

IV

Though not representing, nor even suggesting, the whole range of sotoba-literature, the foregoing texts will sufficiently indicate the quality of its philosophical interest. The inscriptions of the *haka*, or tombs, have another kind of interest; but before treating of these, a few words should be said about the tombs themselves. I cannot attempt detail, because any description of the various styles of such monuments would require a large and profusely illustrated volume; while the study of their sculptures belongs to the enormous subject of Buddhist iconography, — foreign to the purpose of this essay.

There are hundreds, — probably thousands, — of different forms of Buddhist funeral monuments, — ranging from the unhewn boulder, with a few ideographs scratched on it, of the poorest village-graveyard, to the complicated turret (*hagékio*) enclosing a shrine with images, and surmounted with a spire of umbrella-shaped disks or parasols (Sanscrit: *tchâtras*), — possibly representing the old Chinese stûpa. The most common class of *haka* are plain. A large number of the

better class have lotos-designs chiselled upon some
part of them : — either the pedestal is sculptured
so as to represent lotos-petals ; or a single blossom
is cut in relief or intaglio on the face of the tablet ;
or — (but this is rare) — a whole lotos-plant,
leaves and flowers, is designed in relief upon one
or two sides of the monument. In the costly
class of tombs symbolizing the Five Buddhist
Elements, the eight-petalled lotos-symbol may be
found repeated, with decorative variations, upon
three or four portions of their elaborate structure.
Occasionally we find beautiful reliefs upon tomb-
stones, — images of Buddhas or Bodhisattvas ;
and not unfrequently a statue of Jizō may be seen
erected beside a grave. But the sculptures of
this class are mostly old ; — the finest pieces in
the Kobudera cemetery, for example, were exe-
cuted between two and three hundred years ago.
Finally I may observe that the family crest or
mon of the dead is cut upon the front of the
tomb, and sometimes also upon the little stone
tank set before it.

The inscriptions very seldom include any texts
from the holy books. On the front of the monument, below the chiselled crest, the kaimyō is

graven, together, perhaps, with a single mystical
character — Sanscrit or Chinese ; on the left side
is usually placed the record of the date of death ;
and on the right, the name of the person or
family erecting the tomb. Such is now, at least,
the ordinary arrangement ; but there are numerous exceptions ; and as the characters are most
often disposed in vertical columns, it is quite easy
to put all the inscriptions upon the face of a very
narrow monument. Occasionally the real name
is also cut upon some part of the stone, — together, perhaps, with some brief record of the
memorable actions of the dead. Excepting the
kaimyō, and the sect-invocation often accompany-
ing it, the inscriptions upon the ordinary class of
tombs are secular in character ; and the real interest of such epigraphy is limited to the kaimyō.
By *kai*-myō (*sîla*-name) is meant the Buddhist
name given to the spirit of the dead, according to
the custom of all sects except the Ikkō or Shinshū.
In a special sense the term *kai*, or sîla, refers to
precepts of conduct [1] ; in a general sense it might

[1] There is a great variety of *sîla* ; — five, eight, and ten for
different classes of laity ; two hundred and fifty for priests ;
— five hundred for nuns, etc., etc.— Be it here observed
that the posthumous Buddhist name given to the dead must
not be studied as referring always to conduct in this world,

be rendered as "salvation by works." But the Shinshū allows no *kai* to any mortal; it does not admit the doctrine of immediate salvation by works, but only by faith in Amida; and the posthumous appellations which it bestows are therefore called not *kai*-myō, but *hō-myō*, or "Law-names."

Before Meiji the social rank occupied by any one during life was suggested by the kaimyō. The use, with a kaimyō, of the two characters reading *in den*, and signifying "temple-dweller," or "mansion-dweller," — or of the more common single character *in*, signifying "temple" or "mansion," was a privilege reserved to the nobility and gentry. Class-distinctions were further indicated by suffixes. *Koji*, — a term partly corresponding to our "lay-brother," — and *Daishi*, "great elder-sister," were honorifically attached to the kaimyō of the samurai and the aristocracy; while the simpler appellations of *Shinshi* and *Shinnyo*, respectively signifying "faithful [believing] man," "faithful woman," followed the

but rather as referring to *sîla* in another world. The *kai-myō* is thus a t?tle of spiritual initiation. — Some Japanese Buddhist sects hold what are called *Ju-Kai-E* (" *sîla*-giving assemblies "), at which the initiated are given *kaimyō* of another sort, — *sîla*-names of admission as neophytes.

kaimyō of the humble. These forms are still used ;
but the distinctions they once maintained have
mostly passed away, and the privilege of the
knightly " *in den,*" and its accompaniments, is
free to any one willing to pay for it. At all
times the words *Dōji* and *Dōnyo* seem to have
been attached to the kaimyō of children. *Dō*,
alone, means a lad, but when combined with *ji* or
nyo it means " child " in the adjectival sense ; —
so that we may render *Dōji* as " Child-son," and
Dōnyo as " Child-daughter."   Children are thus
called who die before reaching their fifteenth year,
— the majority-year by the old samurai code ;
a lad of fifteen being deemed fit for war-service.
In the case of children who die within a year
after birth, the terms *Gaini* and *Gainyo* occasionally replace *Dōji* and *Dōnyo*. The syllable *Gai*
here represents a Chinese character meaning
" suckling."

　Different Buddhists sects have different form-
ulas for the composition of the kaimyō and
its addenda ; —but this subject would require a
whole special treatise ; and I shall mention only
a few sectarian customs. The Shingon sect sometimes put a Sanscrit character — the symbol of
a Buddha — before their kaimyō ; — the Shin

head theirs with an abbreviation of the holy
name Sakyamuni; — the Nichiren often preface
their inscriptions with the famous invocation,
Namu myō hō rengé kyō ("Hail to the Sutra of
the Lotos of the Good Law!"), — sometimes
followed by the words *Senzo daidai* ("forefathers of the generations"); — the Jōdo, like
the Ikkō, use an abbreviation of the name Sakyamuni, or, occasionally, the invocation *Namu
Amida Butsu!* — and they compose their four-
character kaimyō with the aid of two ideographs
signifying "honour" or "fame;" — the Zen
sect contrive that the first and the last character
of the kaimyō, when read together, shall form a
particular Buddhist term, or mystical phrase, —
except when the kaimyō consists of only two
characters.

Probably the word "mansion" in kaimyō-in-
scriptions would suggest to most Western readers
the idea of heavenly mansions. But the fancy
would be at fault. The word has no celestial
signification; yet the history of its epitaphic use
is curious enough. Anciently, at the death of
any illustrious man, a temple was erected for the
special services due to his spirit, and also for the
conservation of relics or memorials of him. Con-

fucianism introduced into Japan the *ihai*, or mortuary tablet, called by the Chinese *shin-shu* ; [1] and a portion of the temple was set apart to serve as a chapel for the *ihai*, and the ancestral cult. Any such memorial temple was called *in*, or " mansion," — doubtless because the august spirit was believed to occupy it at certain periods; — and the term yet survives in the names of many celebrated Buddhist temples, — such as the Chion-In, of Kyōtō. With the passing of time, this custom was necessarily modified ; for as privileges were extended and aristocracies multiplied, the erection of a separate temple to each notable presently became impossible. Buddhism met the difficulty by conferring upon every individual of distinction the posthumous title of *in-den*, — and affixing to this title the name of an imaginary temple or "mansion." So to-day, in the vast majority of kaimyō, the character *in* refers only to the temple that would have been built had circumstance permitted, but now exists only in the pious desire of those who love and reverence the departed.

Nevertheless the poetry of these *in*-names does

---

[1] That is, according to the Japanese reading of the Chinese characters.

TOMB IN KOBUDERA CEMETERY

(*The relief represents Seishi Bosatsu — Bodhisattva Mahâsthâma — in
meditation. It is 187 years old. The white patches on the
surface are lichen growths*)

possess some real meaning. They are nearly all of them names such as would be given to real Buddhist temples, — names of virtues and sanctities and meditations, — names of ecstasies and powers and splendors and luminous immeasurable unfoldings, — names of all ways and means of escape from the Six States of Existence and the sorrow of "peopling the cemeteries again and again."

The general character and arrangement of kaimyō can best be understood by the aid of a few typical specimens. The first example is from a beautiful tomb in the cemetery of Kobudera, which is sculptured with a relief representing the Bodhisattva Mahâsthâma (Seishi Bosatsu) meditating. All the text in this instance has been cut upon the face of the monument, to left and right of the icon. Transliterated into Romaji it reads thus : —

(Kaimyō.)

Tei-Shō-In, HŌ-SŌ MYŌ-SHIN, *Daishi.*

(Record.)

—Shōtoku Ni, Jin shin Shimotsuki, jiu-ku nichi.

[Translation : —

— Great Elder-Sister, WONDERFUL-REALITY-APPEARING-AT-THE-WINDOW-OF-LAW, *dwelling in the Mansion of the Pine of Chastity.*

—The nineteenth day of the Month of Frost,[1] second year of Shōtoku,[2] — the year being under the Dragon of Elder Water.]

For the sake of clearness, I have printed the posthumous name proper (*Hō-sō Myō-shin*) in small capitals, and the rest in italics. The first three characters of the inscription, — *Tei-Shō-In,* — form the name of the temple, or " mansion." The pine, both in religious and secular poetry, is a symbol of changeless conditions of good, because it remains freshly-green in all seasons. The use of the term " Reality " in the kaimyō indicates the state of unity with the Absolute ; — by " Window-of-Law " (Law here signifying the Buddha-state) must be understood that exercise of virtue through which even in this existence some percep-

---

[1] By the old calendar, the eleventh month was the Month of Frost.

[2] The second year of the period Shōtoku corresponds to 1712 A. D. — (For the meaning of the phrase " Dragon of Elder Water " the reader will do well to consult Professor Rein's *Japan,* pp. 434–436.)

tion of Infinite Truth may be obtained. I have already explained the final word, *Daishi* ("great elder-sister").

Less mystical, but not less beautiful, is this Nichiren kaimyō sculptured upon the grave of a young samurai: —

> *Ko-shin In, Ken-dō Nichi-ki, Koji.*

[*Koji,* —

Bright-Sun-on-the-Way-of-the-Wise, in the Mansion of Luminous Mind.][1]

On the same stone is carven the kaimyō of the wife: —

> *Shin-kyō In, Myō-en Nichi-ko, Daishi.*

[*Daishi,* —

Spherically-Wondrous-Sunbeam, in the Mansion of the Mirror of the Heart.]

Perhaps the reader will now be able to find interest in the following selection of kaimyō, translated for me by Japanese scholars. The inscriptions are of various rites and epochs; but I have arranged them only by class and sex: —

[1] This beautiful kaimyō is identical with that placed upon the monument of my dear friend Nishida, buried in the Nichiren cemetery of Chōmanji, in Matsué.

[MASCULINE KAIMYŌ.]

Koji, —

Law-Nature-Eternally-Complete, in the Mansion of the Mirror of Light.

Koji, —

Lone-Moon-above-Snowy-Peak, in the Mansion of Quiet Light.

Koji, —

Wonderful-Radiance-of-Luminous-Sound, in the Mansion of the Day-dawn of Mind.

Koji, —

Pure-Lotos-bloom-of-the-Heart, in the Mansion of Shining Beginnings.

Koji, —

Real-Earnestness-Self-sufficing-within, in the Mansion of Mystery-Penetration.

Koji, —

Wonderful - Brightness-of-the-Clouds-of-Law, in the Mansion of Wisdom-Illumination.

Koji, —

Law-Echo-proclaiming-Truth, in the Mansion of Real Zeal.

Koji, —

Ocean-of-Reason-Calmly-Full, in the Mansion of Self-Nature.

Koji, —
   Effective - Benevolence - Hearing - with - Pure-Heart-the-Supplications-of-the-Poor, — *dwelling in the Mansion of the Virtue of Pity*.

Koji, —
   Perfect - Enlightenment - beaming - tranquil - Glory, — *in the Mansion of Supreme Comprehension*.

Koji, —
   Autumnal-Prospect-Clear-of-Cloud, — *of the Household of Sakyamuni*, — *in the Mansion of the Obedient Heart*.

Koji, —
   Illustrious-Brightness, — *of the Household of the Buddha*, — *in the Mansion of Conspicuous Virtue*.

Koji, —
   Daily-Peace-Home-Prospering, in the Mansion of Spherical Completeness.

Shinshi, —
   Prosperity - wide - shining - as - the - Moon - of - Autumn.

Shinshi, —
   Vow-abiding·wondrously-without-fault.

Shinshi, —
Vernal-Mountain-bathed-in-the - Light - of - the Law.

Shinshi, —
Waking-to-Dhyâna-at-the- Bell - Peal - of - the Wondrous-Dawn.

Shinshi, —
Winter-Mountain-Chastity-Mind.[1]

[FEMININE KAIMYŌ]

Daishi, —
Moon-Dawn-of-the-Mountain-of-Light, dwelling in the August Mansion of Self-witness.[2]

---

[1] Signifying : — " believing man of mind as chastely pure as the snow upon a peak in winter."

[2] This is the kaimyō of the lady for whose sake the temple of Kobudera was built ; and the words "Mansion of Self-witness" here refer to the temple itself, which is thus named (*Ji-Shō In*). The Chinese text reads : — Ji-Shō-In den, Kwo-zan Kyō-kei, Daishi," — literally, " Great Elder - Sister, Dawn-Katsura-of-Luminous-Mountain, dwelling in the August Mansion of Self-witness." The katsura (*olea fragrans*) is a tree mysteriously connected, in Japanese poetical fancy, with the moon ; and its name is often used, as here, to signify the moon. *Katsura-no-hana*, or " katsura-flower " is a poetical term for moonlight. — This kaimyō is remarkable in having the honorific term " August " prefixed to the name of the mansion or temple, — a sign of the high rank of the dead lady. The full date

Daishi, —

Wondrous-Lotos-of-Fleckless-Light, in the Mansion of the Moonlike Heart.

Daishi, —

Wonderful-Chastity-Responding-with-Pure-Mind-to-the-Summons-of-Duty, — in the Mansion of the Great Sea of Compassion.

Daishi, —

Lotos-Heart-of-Wondrous-Apparition, — in the Mansion of Luminous Perfume.

Daishi, —

Clear-Light-of-the-Spotless-Moon, in the Mansion of Spring-time-Eve.

Kaishi, —

Pure-Mind-as-a-Sun-of-Compassion, in the Mansion of Real Light.

Daishi, —

Wondrous-Lotos-of-Fragrance-Etherial, in the Mansion of Law-Nature.

Shinnyo, —

Rejoicing-in-the-Way-of-the-Infinite.

inscribed is "twenty-eighth day of Mid-Autumn" (the old eighth month) "of the seventeenth year of Kwansei" (1640 A. D.)

Shinnyo, —

   *Excellent - Courage - to - follow-Wisdom-to-the-
   End.*

Shinnyo, —

   Winter-Moon-shedding-purest-Light.

Shinnyo, —

   *Luminous - Shadow - in - the-Plumflower-Cham-
   ber.*

Shinnyo, —

   Virtue-fragrant-as-the-Odor-of-the-Lotos.

[CHILDREN'S KAIMYŌ. — MALE.]

Dai-Dōji,[1] —

   *Instantly - Attaining - to - the - Perfect - Peace,
   dwelling in the August Mansion of Purity.*

Dai-Dōji,[2] —

   *Permeating-Lucidity-of-the-Pure-Grove, dwel-
   ling in the August Mansion of Blossom-
   Fragrance.*

[1] The prefix *dai* (great) before the ordinary term *dōji* (male child) is of rare occurrence. Probably the lad was of princely birth. The grave is in a reserved part of the Kobu-dera cemetery; and the year-date of death is " the fourth of Enkyō " — corresponding to 1747.

[2] The tomb bearing this kaimyō is set beside that in-scribed with the kaimyō preceding. Probably the boys

Gaini, —
  Frost-Glimmer.

Dōji, —
  Dewy-Light.

Dōji, —
  Dream-of-Spring.

Dōji, —
  Spring-Frost.

Dōji, —
  Ethereal-Nature.

Dōji, —
  Rain-of-the-Law-from-translucent-Clouds.

[CHILDREN'S KAIMYŌ. — FEMALE.]

Dai-Dōnyo, [1] —
  *Bright-Shining-Height-of-Wisdom, dwelling in
  the August Mansion of Fragrant Trees.*

were brothers. In both instances we have the honorific
prefix "dai," and the term "August" qualifying the mansion-name. The year-date of death is "the second of
Kwan-en" (1749).

  [1] Probably a princely child, — sister apparently of the
highborn boys before referred to. She is buried beside
them in Kobudera. Observe here again the use of the prefix *dai*, — this time before the term *dōnyo*, "child-girl" or

Gainyo, —
  Snowy-Bubble.

Gainyo, —
  Shining-Phantasm.

Dōnyo, —
  Plumflower-Light.

Dōnyo, —
  Dream-Phantasm.

Dōnyo, —
  Chaste-Spring.

Dōnyo —
  Wisdom-Mirror-of-Flawless-Appearing.

Dōnyo, —
  Wondrous-Excellence-of-Fragrant-Snow.

After having studied the sotoba-texts previously cited, the reader should be able to divine the meaning of most of the kaimyō above given. At all events he will understand such frequently-

---

" child-daughter." Perhaps the *dai* here would be better rendered by "grand" than by "great." Notice that the term "August" precedes the mansion-name in this case also. The date of death is given as "the sixth year of Hōreki" (1756).

repeated terms as "Moon," "Lotos," "Law."
But he may be puzzled by other expressions; and
some further explanation will, perhaps, not be
unwelcome.

Besides expressing a pious hope for the higher
happiness of the departed, or uttering some
assurance of special conditions in the spiritual
world, a great number of kaimyō also refer,
directly or indirectly, to the character of the vanished personality. Thus a man of widely-recog-
nized integrity and strong moral purpose, may —
like my dead friend — be not unfitly named:
"Bright - Sun - on - the - Way - of - the - Wise." The
child-daughter or the young wife, especially remembered for sweetness of character, may be com-
memorated by some such posthumous name as
"Plumflower-Light," or "Luminous-Shadow-of-
the-Plumflower-Chamber;"— the word "plum-
flower" in either case at once suggesting the
quality of the virtue of the dead, because this
blossom in Japan is the emblem of feminine
moral charm, — more particularly faithfulness to
duty and faultless modesty. Again, the memory
of any person noted for deeds of charity may
be honoured by such a kaimyō as, "Effective-
Benevolence Listening - with - Pure- Heart-to-the-

Supplications - of - the - Poor."   Finally I may
observe that the kaimyō-terms expressing altitude, luminosity, and fragrance, have most often
a moral-exemplary signification.   But in all
countries epitaphic literature has its conventional
hypocrisies or extravagances.   Buddhist kaimyō
frequently contain a great deal of religious
flattery ; and beautiful posthumous names are
often given to those whose lives were the reverse
of beautiful.

When we find among feminine kaimyō such
appellations as " Wondrous-Lotos," or "Beautiful-
as-the-Lotos-of-the-Dawn," we may be sure in
the generality of cases that the charm, to which
reference is so made, was ethical only.   Yet there
are exceptions ; and the more remarkable of these
are furnished by the kaimyō of children.   Names
like " Dream-of-Spring," " Radiant-Phantasm,"
" Snowy-Bubble," do actually refer to the lost
form, — or at least to the supposed parental idea
of vanished beauty and grace.   But such names
also exemplify a peculiar consolatory application
of the Buddhist doctrine of Impermanency.   We
might say that through the medium of these
kaimyō the bereaved are thus soothed in the
loftiest language of faith : — " Beautiful and brief

was the being of your child, — a dream of spring,
a radiant passing vision, — a snowy bubble.   But
in the order of eternal law all forms must pass ;
material permanency there is none : only the
divine Absolute dwelling in every being, — only
the Buddha in the heart of each of us, — forever
endures.   Be this great truth at once your com-
fort and your hope ! "

Extraordinary examples of the retrospective
significance sometimes given to posthumous
names, are furnished by the kaimyō of the
Forty-Seven Rōnin buried at Sengakuji in
Tōkyō.   (Their story is now well-known to all
the English-reading world through Mitford's
eloquent and sympathetic version of it in the
" Tales of Old Japan.")   The noteworthy peculiarity of these kaimyō is that each contains
the two words, " dagger " and " sword," — used
in a symbolic sense, but having also an appro-
priate military suggestiveness.   Ōïshi Kuranosuké
Yoshiwo, the leader, is alone styled *Koji ;* — the
kaimyō of his followers have the humbler suffix
Shinshi.   Ōïshi's kaimyō reads : — " *Dagger-of-
Emptiness-and-stainless-Sword, in the Mansion
of Earnest Loyalty.*"   I need scarcely call atten-

tion to the historic meaning of the mansion-name.
Three of the kaimyō of his followers will serve
as examples of the rest. That of Masé Kyudayu
Masaake is : — " *Dagger-of-Fame-and-Sword-of-
the-Way* [*or Doctrine.*] " The kaimyō of Ōïshi
Sezayémon Nobukiyo is : — " *Dagger-of-Mag-
nanimity - and - Sword - of - Virtue.*" And the
kaimyō of Horibei Yasubei is : — " *Dagger-of-
Cloud-and Sword-of-Brightness.*"

The first and the last of these four kaimyō will
be found obscure ; and several more of the forty-
seven inscriptions are equally enigmatic at first
sight. Usually in a kaimyō the word " Emptiness," or " Void," signifies the Buddhist state of
absolute spiritual purity, — the state of Unconditioned Being. But in the kaimyō of Ōïshi
Kuranosuké the meaning of it, though purely
Buddhist, is very different. By " emptiness "
here, we must understand " illusion," " unreality," — and the full meaning of the phrase " dag-
ger-emptiness " is : — " *Wisdom that, seeing the
emptiness of material forms, pierces through
illusion as a dagger.*" In Horibei Yasubei's kaimyō we must similarly render the word " cloud "
by illusion ; and " Dagger-of-Cloud " should be
interpreted, " *Illusion-penetrating Dagger of Wis-*

dom."   The wisdom that perceives the emptiness of phenomena, is the sharply-dividing, or distinguishing wisdom, — is *Myō-kwan-ʐatsu-chi* (Pratyavekshana-gñâna).

V

Possibly I have presumed too much upon the patience of my readers ; yet I feel that these studies can yield scarcely more than the glimpse of a subject wide and deep as a sea.   If they should arouse any Western interest in the philosophy and the poetry of Buddhist epitaphic literature, then they will certainly have accomplished all that I could reasonably hope.

Not improbably I shall be accused, as I have been on other occasions, of trying to make Buddhist texts "more beautiful than they are."   This charge usually comes from persons totally ignorant of the originals, and betrays a spirit of disingenuousness with which I have no sympathy. Whoever confesses religion to have been a developing influence in the social and moral history of races, — whoever grants that respect is due to

convictions which have shaped the nobler courses
of human conduct for thousands of years, —
whoever acknowledges that in any great religion
something of eternal truth must exist, — will hold
it the highest duty of a translator to interpret the
concepts of an alien faith as generously as he
would wish his own thoughts or words interpreted
by his fellow-men.   In the rendering of Chinese
sentences this duty presents itself under a peculiar
aspect.   Any attempt at literal translation would
result in the production either of nonsense, or of a
succession of ideas totally foreign to far-Eastern
thought.   The paramount necessity in treating
such texts is to discover and to expound the
thought conveyed to Oriental minds by the
original ideographs, — which are very different
things indeed from " written words."   The translations given in this essay were made by Japanese
scholars, and, in their present form, have the
approval of competent critics.

As I write these lines a full moon looks into
my study over the trees of the temple-garden,
and brings me the recollection of a little Buddhist
poem : —

" From the foot of the mountain, many are the paths ascending in shadow ; but from the cloudless summit all who climb behold the self-same Moon."

The reader who knows the truth shrined in this little verse will not regret an hour passed with me among the tombs of Kobudera.

Frogs

Frogs

"With hands resting upon the floor, reverentially you repeat your poem, O frog ! "

Ancient Poem.

I

FEW of the simpler sense-impressions of travel remain more intimately and vividly associated with the memory of a strange land than sounds, — sounds of the open country. Only the traveller knows how Nature's voices — voices of forest and river and plain — vary according to zone ; and it is nearly always some local peculiarity of their tone or character that appeals to feeling and penetrates into memory, — giving us the sensation of the foreign and the far-away. In Japan this sensation is especially aroused by the music of insects, — hemiptera uttering a sound-language wonderfully different from that of their Western congeners. To a lesser degree the exotic accent is noticeable also in the chanting of Japanese frogs, — though the sound impresses itself upon remembrance rather

by reason of its ubiquity. Rice being cultivated
all over the country, — not only upon mountain-
slopes and hill-tops, but even within the limits of
the cities, — there are flushed levels everywhere,
and everywhere frogs. No one who has travelled
in Japan will forget the clamor of the ricefields.

Hushed only during the later autumn and brief
winter, with the first wakening of spring waken
all the voices of the marsh-lands, — the infinite
bubbling chorus that might be taken for the
speech of the quickening soil itself. And the
universal mystery of life seems to thrill with a
peculiar melancholy in that vast utterance —
heard through forgotten thousands of years
by forgotten generations of toilers, but doubtless
older by myriad ages than the race of man.

Now this song of solitude has been for centuries a favorite theme with Japanese poets; but
the Western reader may be surprised to learn that
it has appealed to them rather as a pleasant sound
than as a nature-manifestation.

Innumerable poems have been written about
the singing of frogs; but a large proportion of
them would prove unintelligible if understood as
referring to common frogs. When the general

chorus of the ricefield finds praise in Japanese
verse, the poet expresses his pleasure only in the
great volume of sound produced by the blending
of millions of little croakings, — a blending which
really has a pleasant effect, well compared to the
lulling sound of the falling of rain. But when
the poet pronounces an individual frog-call melodious, he is not speaking of the common frog of
the ricefields. Although most kinds of Japanese
frogs are croakers, there is one remarkable excep-
tion — (not to mention tree-frogs), — the *kajika*,
or true singing-frog of Japan. To say that it
croaks would be an injustice to its note, which is
sweet as the chirrup of a song-bird. It used to be
called *kawazu;* but as this ancient appellation
latterly became confounded in common parlance
with *haeru,* the general name for ordinary frogs,
it is now called only *kajika*. The *kajika* is kept
as a domestic pet, and is sold in Tōkyō by several
insect-merchants. It is housed in a peculiar cage,
the lower part of which is a basin containing sand
and pebbles, fresh water and small plants; the
upper part being a framework of fine wire-gauze.
Sometimes the basin is fitted up as a *ko-niwa,*
or model landscape-garden. In these times the
kajika is considered as one of the singers of spring

and summer; but formerly it was classed witl. the melodists of autumn; and people used to make autumn-trips to the country for the mere pleasure of hearing it sing. And just as various places used to be famous for the music of particular varieties of night-crickets, so there were places celebrated only as haunts of the kajika. The following were especially noted : —

Tamagawa and Ōsawa-no-Iké, — a river and a lake in the province of Yamashiro.

Miwagawa, Asukagawa, Sawogawa, Furu-no-Yamada, and Yoshinogawa, — all in the province of Yamato.

Koya-no-Iké, — in Settsu.

Ukinu-no-Iké, — in Iwami.

Ikawa-no-Numa, — in Kōzuké.

Now it is the melodious cry of the kajika, or kawazu, which is so often praised in far-Eastern verse ; and, like the music of insects, it is mentioned in the oldest extant collections of Japanese poems. In the preface to the famous anthology called *Kokinshū*, compiled by Imperial Decree during the fifth year of the period of Engi (A. D. 905), the poet Ki-no-Tsurayuki, chief editor of the work, makes these interesting observations : —

— " The poetry of Japan has its roots in the human heart, and thence has grown into a multi-form utterance. Man in this world, having a thousand millions of things to undertake and to complete, has been moved to express his thoughts and his feelings concerning all that he sees and hears. When we hear the *uguisu*[1] singing among flowers, and the voice of the kawazu which inhabits the waters, what mortal [*lit.: 'who among the living that lives'*] does not compose poems ? "

The kawazu thus referred to by Tsurayuki is of course the same creature as the modern kajika : no common frog could have been mentioned as a songster in the same breath with that wonderful bird, the uguisu. And no common frog could have inspired any classical poet with so pretty a fancy as this : —

> Té wo tsuité,
> Uta moshi-aguru,
> Kawazu kana !

" With hands resting on the ground, reverentially you repeat your poem, O frog ! " The charm of this little verse can best be understood by those familiar with the far-Eastern etiquette of posture

---

[1] *Cettia cantans,* — the Japanese nightingale.

II

while addressing a superior, — kneeling, with the body respectfully inclined, and hands resting upon the floor, with the fingers pointing outwards.[1]

It is scarcely possible to determine the antiquity of the custom of writing poems about frogs; but in the *Manyōshū*, dating back to the middle of the eighth century, there is a poem which suggests that even at that time the river Asuka had long been famous for the singing of its frogs : —

> Ima mo ka mo
> Asuka no kawa no
> Yū sarazu
> Kawazu naku sé no
> Kiyoku aruran.

" Still clear in our day remains the stream of Asuka, where the kawazu nightly sing." We find also in the same anthology the following curious reference to the singing of frogs : —

> Omoboyezu
> Kimaseru kimi wo,
> Sasagawa no
> Kawazu kikasezu
> Kayeshi tsuru kamo !

---

[1] Such, at least, is the posture prescribed by the old etiquette for *men*. But the rules were very complicated, and varied somewhat according to rank as well as to sex. Women usually turn the fingers inward instead of outward when assuming this posture.

"Unexpectedly I received the august visit of my lord. . . . Alas, that he should have returned without hearing the frogs of the river Sawa!" And in the *Rokujōshū*, another ancient compilation, are preserved these pleasing verses on the same theme : —

Tamagawa no
Hito wo mo yogizu
Naku kawazu,
Kono yū kikéba
Oshiku ya wa aranu?

"Hearing to-night the frogs of the Jewel River [or Tamagawa], that sing without fear of man, how can I help loving the passing moment?"

II

Thus it appears that for more than eleven hundred years the Japanese have been making poems about frogs; and it is at least possible that verses on this subject, which have been preserved in the *Manyōshū*, were composed even earlier than the eighth century. From the oldest classical period to the present day, the theme has never ceased to be a favorite one with poets of all ranks.   A fact noteworthy in this relation is that the first poem written in the measure called *hokku*, by the famous Bashō, was about frogs. The triumph of this extremely brief form of verse — (three lines of 5, 7, and 5 syllables respectively) — is to create one complete sensation-picture ; and Bashō's original accomplishes the feat, — difficult, if not impossible, to repeat in English : —

> Furu iké ya,
> Kawazu tobikomu,
> Midzu no oto.

("Old pond — frogs jumping in — sound of water.")   An immense number of poems about frogs were subsequently written in this measure. Even at the present time professional men of letters amuse themselves by making short poems on frogs.   Distinguished among these is a young poet known to the Japanese literary world by the pseudonym of "Roséki," who lives in Ōsaka and keeps in the pond of his garden hundreds of singing frogs.   At fixed intervals he invites all his poet-friends to a feast, with the proviso that each must compose, during the entertainment, one poem about the inhabitants of the pond.   A collection of the verses thus obtained was privately printed in the spring of 1897, with funny pictures of frogs decorating the covers and illustrating the text.

But unfortunately it is not possible through English translation to give any fair idea of the range and character of the literature of frogs. The reason is that the greater number of compositions about frogs depend chiefly for their literary value upon the untranslatable, — upon local allusions, for example, incomprehensible outside of Japan; upon puns; and upon the use of words with double or even triple meanings. Scarcely two or three in every one hundred poems can bear translation. So I can attempt little more than a few general observations.

That love-poems should form a considerable proportion of this curious literature will not seem strange to the reader when he is reminded that the lovers' trysting-hour is also the hour when the frog-chorus is in full cry, and that, in Japan at least, the memory of the sound would be associated with the memory of a secret meeting in almost any solitary place. The frog referred to in such poems is not usually the kajika. But frogs are introduced into love-poetry in countless

clever ways.   I can give two examples of modern
popular compositions of this kind.   The first contains an allusion to the famous proverb, — *I no
naka no kawazu daikai wo shirazu:* "The frog
in the well knows not the great sea."   A person
quite innocent of the ways of the world is compared to a frog in a well; and we may suppose
the speaker of the following lines to be some
sweet-hearted country-girl, answering an ungen-
erous remark with very pretty tact: —

*Laugh me to scorn if you please; — call me your
    "frog-in-the-well":*
*Flowers fall into my well; and its water mirrors
    the moon!*

The second poem is supposed to be the utterance
of a woman having good reason to be jealous: —

*Dull as a stagnant pond you deemed the mind of
    your mistress;*
*But the stagnant pond can speak: you shall hear
    the cry of the frog!*

Outside of love-poems there are hundreds of
verses about the common frogs of ponds or ricefields.   Some refer chiefly to the volume of the
sound that the frogs make: —

Hearing the frogs of the ricefields, methinks that the water sings.

As we flush the ricefields of spring, the frog-song flows with the water.

From ricefield to ricefield they call : unceasing the challenge and answer.

Ever as deepens the night, louder the chorus of pond-frogs.

So many the voices of frogs that I cannot but wonder if the pond be not wider at night than by day !

Even the rowing boats can scarce proceed, so thick the clamor of the frogs of Horiè !

The exaggeration of the last verse is of course intentional, and in the original not uneffective. In some parts of the world — in the marshes of Florida and of southern Louisiana, for example, — the clamor of the frogs at certain seasons resembles the roaring of a furious sea ; and whoever has heard it can appreciate the fancy of sound as obstacle.

Other poems compare or associate the sound
made by frogs with the sound of rain:—

*The song of the earliest frogs,—fainter than
falling of rain.*

*What I took for the falling of rain is only the
singing of frogs.*

*Now I shall dream, lulled by the patter of rain
and the song of the frogs.*

Other poems, again, are intended only as tiny
pictures,— thumb-nail sketches,— such as this
hokku, —

*Path between ricefields ; frogs jumping away
to right and left ; —*

—or this, which is a thousand years old :—

*Where the flowers of the yamabuki are imaged
in the still marsh-water, the voice of the kawazu is heard ; —*

— or the following pretty fancy :—

*Now sings the frog, and the voice of the frog
is perfumed ; —for into the shining stream the
cherry-petals fall.*

The last two pieces refer, of course, to the true singing frog.

Many short poems are addressed directly to the frog itself, — whether kaeru or kajika. There are poems of melancholy, of affection, of humor, of religion, and even of philosophy among these. Sometimes the frog is likened to a spirit resting on a lotos-leaf; sometimes, to a priest repeating sûtras for the sake of the dying flowers; sometimes to a pining lover; sometimes to a host receiving travellers; sometimes to a blasphemer, "always beginning" to say something against the gods, but always afraid to finish it. Most of the following examples are taken from the recent book of frog-poems published by Roséki; — each paragraph of my prose rendering, it should be remembered, represents a distinct poem : —

Now all the guests being gone, why still thus respectfully sitting, O frog?

So resting your hands on the ground, do you welcome the Rain, O frog?

You disturb in the ancient well the light of the stars, O frog!

Sleepy the sound of the rain; but your voice makes me dream, O frog!

Always beginning to say something against the great Heaven, O frog!

You have learned that the world is void: you never look at it as you float, O frog!

Having lived in clear-rushing mountain-streams, never can your voice become stagnant, O frog!

The last pleasing conceit shows the esteem in which the superior vocal powers of the kajika are held.

III

I thought it strange that out of hundreds of frog-poems collected for me I could not discover a single mention of the coldness and clamminess of the frog.   Except a few jesting lines about the queer attitudes sometimes assumed by the creature, the only reference to its uninviting qualities that I could find was the mild remark,

Seen in the daytime, how uninteresting you are, O frog!

While wondering at this reticence concerning the chilly, slimy, flaccid nature of frogs, it all at once occurred to me that in other thousands of Japanese poems which I had read there was a total absence of allusions to tactual sensations. Sensations of colors, sounds, and odors were rendered with exquisite and surprising delicacy; but sensations of taste were seldom mentioned, and sensations of touch were absolutely ignored. I asked myself whether the reason for this reticence or indifference should be sought in the particular temperament or mental habit of the race; but I have not yet been able to decide the question. Remembering that the race has been living for ages upon food which seems tasteless to the Western palate, and that impulses to such action as hand-clasping, embracing, kissing, or other physical display of affectionate feeling, are really foreign to far-Eastern character, one is tempted to the theory that gustatory and tactual sensations, pleasurable and otherwise, have been less highly evolved with the Japanese than with us. But there is much evidence against such a theory; and the triumphs of Japanese handicraft assure us of an almost incomparable delicacy of touch developed in special directions. Whatever be the physiological meaning of the phenomenon, its moral meaning is of most importance. So far as I have been able to judge, Japanese poetry usually ignores the inferior qualities of sensation, while making the subtlest of appeals to those superior qualities which we call æsthetic. Even if representing nothing else, this fact represents the healthiest and happiest attitude toward Nature. Do not we Occidentals shrink from many purely natural impressions by reason of repulsion developed through a morbid tactual sensibility? The question is at least worth considering. Ignoring or mastering such repulsion, — accepting naked Nature as she is, always lovable when understood, — the Japanese discover beauty where we blindly imagine ugliness or formlessness or loathsomeness, — beauty in insects, beauty in stones, beauty in frogs. Is the fact without significance that they alone have been able to make artistic use of the form of the centipede? . . . You should see my Kyōtō tobacco-pouch, with centipedes of gold running over its figured leather like ripplings of fire!

Of Moon-Desire

Of Moon-Desire

1

HE was two years old when — as ordained in the law of perpetual recurrence — he asked me for the Moon.

Unwisely I protested, —

" The Moon I cannot give you because it is too high up. I cannot reach it."

He answered : —

" By taking a very long bamboo, you probably could reach it, and knock it down."

I said, —

" There is no bamboo long enough."

He suggested : —

" By standing on the ridge of the roof of the house, you probably could poke it with the bamboo."

— Whereat I found myself constrained to make some approximately truthful statements concerning the nature and position of the Moon.

This set me thinking. I thought about the strange fascination that brightness exerts upon living creatures in general, — upon insects and fishes and birds and mammals, — and tried to account for it by some inherited memory of brightness as related to food, to water, and to freedom. I thought of the countless generations of children who have asked for the Moon, and of the generations of parents who have laughed at the asking. And then I entered into the following meditation : —

Have we any right to laugh at the child's wish for the Moon ? No wish could be more natural; and as for its incongruity, — do not we, children of a larger growth, mostly nourish wishes quite as innocent, — longings that if realized could only work us woe, — such as desire for the continuance after death of that very sense-life, or individuality, which once deluded us all into wanting to play with the Moon, and often subsequently deluded us in far less pleasant ways ?

Now foolish as may seem, to merely empirical reasoning, the wish of the child for the Moon, I have an idea that the highest wisdom commands us to wish for very much more than the Moon,

— even for more than the Sun and the Morning-Star and all the Host of Heaven.

II

I remember when a boy lying on my back in the grass, gazing into the summer blue above me, and wishing that I could melt into it, — become a part of it. For these fancies I believe that a religious tutor was innocently responsible : he had tried to explain to me, because of certain dreamy questions, what he termed " the folly and the wickedness of pantheism," — with the result that I immediately became a pantheist, at the tender age of fifteen. And my imaginings presently led me not only to want the sky for a playground, but also to become the sky !

Now I think that in those days I was really close to a great truth, — touching it, in fact, without the faintest suspicion of its existence. I mean the truth that the wish *to become* is reasonable in direct ratio to its largeness, — or, in other words, that the more you wish to be, the wiser you are ; while the wish *to have* is apt to be foolish in proportion to its largeness. Cosmic law permits

us very few of the countless things that we wish
to have, but will help us to become all that we
can possibly wish to be.   Finite, and in so much
feeble, is the wish to have : but infinite in puis-
sance is the wish to become ; and every mortal
wish to become must eventually find satisfaction.
By wanting to be, the monad makes itself the
elephant, the eagle, or the man.   By wanting to
be, the man should become a god.   Perhaps on
this tiny globe, lighted only by a tenth-rate yellow sun, he will not have time to become a god ;
but who dare assert that his wish cannot project
itself to mightier systems illuminated by vaster
suns, and there reshape and invest him with the
forms and powers of divinity ?   Who dare even
say that his wish may not expand him beyond
the Limits of Form, and make him one with
Omnipotence ?   And Omnipotence, without asking, can have much brighter and bigger play-
things than the Moon.

Probably everything is a mere question of wishing, — providing that we wish, not to have, but to
be.   Most of the sorrow of life certainly exists
because of the wrong kind of wishing and because
of the contemptible pettiness of the wishes.   Even
to wish for the absolute lordship and possession

of the entire earth were a pitifully small and
vulgar wish. We must learn to nourish very
much bigger wishes than that! My faith is that
we must wish to become the total universe with
its thousands of millions of worlds, — and more
than the universe, or a myriad universes, — and
more even than Space and Time.

III

Possibly the power for such wishing must
depend upon our comprehension of the ghostliness of substance. Once men endowed with
spirit all forms and motions and utterances of
Nature: stone and metal, herb and tree, cloud
and wind, — the lights of heaven, the murmur-
ing of leaves and waters, the echoes of the hills,
the tumultuous speech of the sea. Then becoming wiser in their own conceit, they likewise became of little faith; and they talked about " the
Inanimate " and " the Inert," — which are non-
existent, — and discoursed of Force as distinct
from Matter, and of Mind as distinct from both.
Yet we now discover that the primitive fancies
were, after all, closer to probable truth. We can-

not indeed think of Nature to-day precisely as did our forefathers; but we find ourselves obliged to think of her in very much weirder ways; and the later revelations of our science have revitalized not a little of the primitive thought, and infused it with a new and awful beauty. And meantime those old savage sympathies with savage Nature that spring from the deepest sources of our being, —always growing with our growth, strengthening with our strength, more and more unfolding with the evolution of our higher sensibilities, — would seem destined to sublime at last into forms of cosmical emotion expanding and responding to infinitude.

Have you never thought about those immemorial feelings? . . . Have you never, when looking at some great burning, found yourself exulting without remorse in the triumph and glory of fire? — never unconsciously coveted the crumbling, splitting, iron-wrenching, granite-cracking force of its imponderable touch? — never delighted in the furious and terrible splendor of its phantasmagories, — the ravening and bickering of its dragons, — the monstrosity of its archings, — the ghostly soaring and flapping of its spires?

Have you never, with a hill-wind pealing in your ears, longed to ride that wind like a ghost, — to scream round the peaks with it, — to sweep the face of the world with it? Or, watching the lifting, the gathering, the muttering rush and thunder-burst of breakers, have you felt no impulse kindred to that giant motion, — no longing to leap with that wild white tossing, and to join in that mighty shout? . . . And all such ancient emotional sympathies with Nature's familiar forces — do they not prelude, with their modern æsthetic developments, the future growth of rarer sympathies with incomparably subtler forces, and of longings to be limited only by our power to know? Know ether — shivering from star to star; — comprehend its sensitivities, its penetrancies, its transmutations; — and sympathies ethereal will evolve. Know the forces that spin the suns; — and already the way has been reached of becoming one with them.

And furthermore, is there no suggestion of such evolvement in the steady widening through all the centuries of the thoughts of their world-priests and poets? — in the later sense of Life-as-Unity absorbing or transforming the ancient childish sense of life-personal? — in the tone of the new rapture in world-beauty, dominating the elder worship of beauty-human ? — in the larger modern joy evoked by the blossoming of dawns, the blossoming of stars, — by all quiverings of color, all shudderings of light ? And is not the thing-in-itself, the detail, the appearance, being ever less and less studied for its mere power to charm, and ever more and more studied as a single character in that Infinite Riddle of which all phenomena are but ideographs ?

Nay ! — surely the time must come when we shall desire to be all that is, all that ever has been known, — the past and the present and the future in one, — all feeling, striving, thinking, joying, sorrowing, — and everywhere the Part, — and everywhere the Whole. And before us, with the waxing of the wish, perpetually the Infinities shall widen.

And I — even I ! — by virtue of that wish, shall become all forms, all forces, all conditions : Ether, Wind, Fire, Water, Earth, — all motion visible or viewless, — all vibration named of light, of color, of sonority, of torrefaction, — all thrillings piercing substance, — all oscillations picturing in blackness, like the goblin-vision of the X-rays.

By virtue of that wish I shall become the Source
of all becoming and of all ceasing, — the Power
that shapes, the Power that dissolves, — creating,
with the shadows of my sleep, the life that shall
vanish with my wakening.   And even as phos-
phor-lampings in currents of midnight sea, so
shall shimmer and pulse and pass, in mine Ocean
of Death and Birth, the burning of billions of
suns, the whirling of trillions of worlds. . . .

IV

— " Well," said the friend to whom I read this
revery, " there is some Buddhism in your fancies
— though you seem to have purposely avoided
several important points of doctrine. For instance, you must know that Nirvana is never to
be reached by wishing, but by *not* wishing. What
you call the ' wish-to-become ' can only help us,
like a lantern, along the darker portions of the
Way.   As for wanting the Moon — I think that
you must have seen many old Japanese pictures
of apes clutching at the reflection of the Moon in
water.   The subject is a Buddhist parable : the
water is the phantom-flux of sensations and ideas ;

the Moon — not its distorted image — is the sole Truth.   And your Western philosopher was really teaching a Buddhist parable when he proclaimed man but a higher kind of ape. For in this world of illusion, man is truly still the ape, trying to seize on water the shadow of the Moon."

— "Ape indeed," I made answer, — " but an ape of gods, — even that divine Ape of the Ramayana who may clutch the Sun!"

Retrospectives

"Murmurs and scents of the Infinite Sea."
— MATTHEW ARNOLD.

First Impressions

I

I WONDER why the emblematical significance of the Composite Photograph has been so little considered by the philosophers of evolution. In the blending and coalescing of the shadows that make it, is there no suggestion of that bioplasmic chemistry which, out of the intermingling of innumerable lives, crystallizes the composite of personality ? Has the superimposition of images upon the sensitized plate no likeness to those endless superimpositions of heredity out of which every individuality must shape itself ? . . . Surely it is a very weird thing, this Composite Photograph, — and hints of things weirder.

Every human face is a living composite of countless faces, — generations and generations of faces superimposed upon the sensitive film of Life

for the great cosmic developing process.   And
any living face, well watched by love or by hate,
will reveal the fact.   The face of friend or sweet-
heart has a hundred different aspects; and you
know that you want, when his or her " likeness "
is taken, to insist upon the reflection of the
dearest of these.   The face of your enemy, — no
matter what antipathy it may excite, — is not in-
variably hateful in itself : you must acknowledge,
to yourself at least, having observed in it moments of an expression the reverse of unworthy.

Probably the ancestral types that try to reproduce themselves in the modulations of facial
expression, are nearly always the more recent ; —
the very ancient having become metamorphosed,
under weight of superimposition, into a blank
underlying   vagueness, — a   mere   protoplasmic
background out of which, except in rare and
monstrous cases, no outline can detach itself.
But in every normal face whole generations of
types do certainly, by turns of mood, make flit-
ting apparition.   Any mother knows this.   Study-
ing day by day the features of her child, she
finds in them variations not to be explained by
simple growth.   Sometimes there is a likeness to
one parent or grandparent; sometimes a likeness

to another, or to remoter kindred; and at rarer
intervals may appear peculiarities of expression
that no member of the family can account for.
(Thus, in darker centuries, the ghastly superstition of the "changeling," was not only possible,
but in a certain sense quite natural.) Through
youth and manhood and far into old age these
mutations continue, — though always more slowly
and faintly, — even while the general character-
istics steadily accentuate; and death itself may
bring into the countenance some strange expression never noticed during life.

II

As a rule we recognize faces by the modes
of expression habitually worn, — by the usually
prevalent character-tones of them, — rather than
by any steady memory of lines.   But no face at all
moments remains exactly the same; and in cases
of exceptional variability the expression does not
suffice for recognition: we have to look for some
fixed peculiarity, some minute superficial detail
independent of physiognomy.   All expression has
but a relative permanency: even in faces the

most strongly marked, its variations may defy estimate. Perhaps the mobility is, within certain limits, in direct ratio to irregularity of feature; — any approach to ideal beauty being also an approach to relative fixity. At all events, the more familiar we become with any common face, the more astonishing the multitude of the transformations we observe in it, — the more indescribable and bewildering its fugitive subtleties of expression. And what are these but the ebb and flow of life ancestral, — under-ripplings in that well-spring unfathomable of personality whose flood is Soul. Perpetually beneath the fluid tissues of flesh the dead are moulding and moving — not singly (for in no phenomenon is there any singleness), but in currents and by surgings. Sometimes there is an eddying of ghosts of love; and the face dawns as if a sunrise lighted it. Sometimes there is a billowing up of ghosts of hate; and the face darkens and distorts like an evil dream, — and we say to the mind behind it, "You are not now *your better self*." But that which we call the self, whether the better or the worse, is a complexity forever shifting the order of its combinations. According to stimulus of hope or fear, of joy or pain, there must vibrate

within every being, at differing rhythms, with
varying oscillation, incalculable tremulosities of
ancestral life. In the calmest normal existence
slumber all the psychical tones of the past, — from
the lurid red of primal sense-impulse to the violet of spiritual aspiration, — even as all known
colours sleep in white light. And over the sensitive living mask, at each strong alternation of the
psychical currents, flit shadowy resurrections of
dead expression.

Seeing faces and their changes, we learn in-
tuitively the relation to our own selves of the
selves that confront us. In very few cases could
we even try to explain how this knowledge
comes, — how we reach those conclusions called,
in common parlance, "first impressions." Faces
are not *read*. The impressions they give are
only *felt*, and have much of the same vague
character as impressions of sound, — making
within us mental states either pleasant or unpleasant or somewhat of both, — evoking now
a sense of danger, now a melting sympathy, occasionally a gentle sadness. And these impressions, though seldom at fault, cannot be very
well explained in words. The reasons of their
accuracy are likewise the reasons of their mys-

tery, — reasons not to be discovered in the narrow range of our personal experience, — reasons very, very much older than we. Could we remember our former lives, we should know more exactly the meaning of our likes and our dislikes. For the truth is that they are superindividual. It is not the individual eye that perceives everything perceived in a face. The dead are the real seers. But as they remain unable to guide us otherwise than by touching the chords of mental pleasure or pain, we can feel the relative meaning of faces only in a dim, though powerful way.

Instinctively, at least, superindividuality is commonly recognized. Hence such phrases as " force of character," " moral force," " personal fascination," " personal magnetism," and others showing that the influence exerted by man upon man is known to be independent of mere physical conditions. Very insignificant bodies have that within them by which formidable bodies are mastered and directed. The flesh-and-blood man is only the visible end of an invisible column of force reaching out of the infinite past into the momentary present, — only the material Symbol of an immaterial host. A contest between even two

wills is a contest of phantom armies. The domination of many personalities by the simple will
of one, — hinting the perception by the compelled
of superior viewless powers behind the compeller,
— is never to be interpreted by the old hypothesis
of soul-equality. Only by scientific psychology
can the mystery of certain formidable characters
be even partly explained ; but any explanation
must rest upon the acceptance, in some form or
other, of the immense evolutional fact of psychical inheritance. And psychical inheritance signifies the super-individual, — pre-existence revived
in compound personality.

Yet, from our ethical standpoint, that superindividuality which we thus unconsciously allow
in the very language used to express psychical
domination, is a lower manifestation. Though
working often for good, the power in itself is of
evil ; and the recognition of it by the subjugated
is not a recognition of higher moral energy, but
of a higher *mental* energy signifying larger evolutional experience of wrong, deeper reserves of
aggressive ingenuity, heavier capacities for the
giving of pain. Called by no matter what eu-
phemistic name, such power is brutal in its origin,
and still allied to those malignities and ferocities

13

shared by man with lower predatory creatures.
But the beauty of the superindividual is revealed
in that rarer power which the dead lend the living
to win trust, to inspire ideals, to create love, to
brighten whole circles of existence with the charm
and wonder of a personality never to be described
save in the language of light and music.

III

Now if we could photographically *decompose* a
composite photograph so as to separate in order
inverse all the impressions interblended to make
it, such process would clumsily represent what
really happens when the image of a strange face
is telegraphed back — like a police-photograph —
from the living retina to the mysterious offices of
inherited memory.   There, with the quickness of
an electric flash, the shadow-face is decomposed
into all the ancestral types combined in it ; and
the resulting verdict of the dead, though rendered
only by indefinable sensation, is more trustworthy
than any written certificate of character could ever
be.   But its trustworthiness is limited to the
potential relation of the individual seen to the

individual seeing.   Upon different minds, according to the delicate balance of personality, — according to the qualitative sum of inherited experience in the psychical composition of the observer, — the same features will make very different impressions.   A face that strongly repels one person may not less strongly attract another, and will produce nearly similar impressions only on groups of emotionally homogeneous natures.   Certainly the fact of this ability to discern in the composition of faces that indefinable something which welcomes or which warns, does suggest the possibility of deciding some laws of ethical physiognomy; but such laws would necessarily be of a very general and simple kind, and their relative value could never equal that of the uneducated personal intuition.

How, indeed, should it be otherwise ?   What science could ever hope to measure the infinite possibilities of psychical combination ?   And the present in every countenance is a recombination of the past; — the living is always a resurrection of the dead.   The sympathies and the fears, the hopes and the repulsions that faces inspire, are but revivals and reiterations, — echoes of sentiency created in millions of minds by immeasurable experience operating through immeasurable time. My friend of this hour, though no more identical with his forefathers than any single ripple of a current is identical with all the ripples that ever preceded it, is nevertheless by soul-composition one with myriads known and loved in other lands and in other lives, — in times recorded and in times forgotten, — in cities that still remain and in cities that have ceased to be, — by thousands of my vanished selves.

Beauty is Memory

Beauty is Memory

I

WHEN you first saw her your heart leaped, and a tingling shocked through all your blood like a gush of electricity. Simultaneously your senses were changed, and long so remained.

That sudden throb was the awakening of your dead ; — and that thrill was made by the swarming and the crowding of them ; — and that change of sense was wrought only by their multitudinous desire, — for which reason it seemed *an intensification.* They remembered having loved a number of young persons somewhat resembling her. But where, or when, they did not recollect. They — (and They, of course, are You) — had drunk of Lethe many times since then.

The true name of the River of Forgetfulness is the River of Death — though you may not find authority for the statement in classical dictionaries.

But the Greek story, that the waters of Lethe bring to weary souls oblivion of the past, is not quite true. One draught will indeed numb and becloud some forms of memory, — will efface the remembrance of dates and names and of other trifling details; — but a million draughts will not produce total oblivion. Even the destruction of the world would not have that result. *Nothing is absolutely forgotten except the non-essential.* The essential can, at most, only be dimmed by the drinking of Lethe.

It was because of billions of billions of memories amassed through trillions of lives, and blended within you into some one vague delicious image, that you came to believe a certain being more beautiful than the sun. The delusion signified that she happened to resemble this composite, — mnemonic shadowing of all the dead women related to the loves of your innumerable lives. And this first part of your experience, when you could not understand, — when you fancied the beloved a witch, and never even dreamed that the witchery might be the work of ghosts, was — the Period of Wonder.

II

Wonder at what ?   At the power and mystery of beauty. (For whether only within yourself, or partly within and partly outside of yourself, it was beauty that you saw, and that made you wonder.) But you will now remember that the beloved seemed lovelier than mortal woman really could be ; — and the how and the why of that seeming are questions of interest.

With the power to see beauty we are born — somewhat, though not altogether, as we are born with the power to perceive color. Most human beings are able to discern something of beauty, or at least of approach to beauty — though the volume of the faculty varies in different individuals more than the volume of a mountain varies from that of a grain of sand. There are men born blind ; but the normal being inherits some ideal of beauty. It may be vivid or it may be vague ; but in every case it represents an accumulation of countless impressions received by the race, — countless fragments of prenatal remembrance crystallized into one composite image within organic memory, where, like the viewless image on a photographic plate awaiting development, it remains awhile in darkness absolute. And just because it is a composite of numberless race-memories of individual attraction, this ideal necessarily represents, in the superior mind, a something above the existing possible, — something never to be realized, much less surpassed, in the present state of humanity.

And what is the relation of this composite, fairer than human possibility, to the illusion of love ? If it be permissible to speak one's imagining of the unimaginable, I can dare a theory. When, in the hour of the ripeness of youth, there is perceived some objective comeliness faintly corresponding to certain outlines of the inherited ideal, at once a wave of emotion ancestral bathes the long-darkened image, defines it, illuminates it, — and so deludes the senses ; — for the sense-reflection of the living objective becomes temporarily blended with the subjective phantasm, — with the beautiful luminous ghost made of centillions of memories. Thus to the lover the common suddenly becomes the impossible, because he really perceives blended with it the superindividual and superhuman. He is much too deeply bewitched by that supernatural to be persuaded of his illusion, by any reasoning. What conquers his will is not the magic of anything living or tangible, but a charm sinuous and fugitive and light as fire, — a spectral snare prepared for him by myriads unthinkable of generations of dead.

So much and no more of theory I venture as to the *how* of the riddle. But what of the *why*, —the reason of the emotion made by this ghostly beauty revived out of the measureless past? What should beauty have to do with a superindividual ecstasy older than all æsthetic feeling? What is the evolutional secret of the fascination of beauty?

I think that an answer can be given. But it will involve the fullest acceptance of this truth: — *There is no such thing as beauty-in-itself.*

All the riddles and contradictions of our æsthetic systems are natural consequences of the delusion that beauty is a something absolute, a transcendental reality, an eternal fact. It is true that the appearance we call beauty is the symbol of a fact, — is the visible manifestation of a development beyond the ordinary, — a bodily evolution more advanced than the existing average.   In like manner what we call grace is a real manifestation of the economy of force.   But since there can be no cosmic limit to evolutional possibilities, there never can be any standards of grace or of beauty that are not relative and essentially transitory ; and there can be no physical ideals, — not even Greek ideals, — that might not in the course of human evolution or of superhuman evolution be so much more than realized as to become vulgarities of form.   An ultimate of beauty is inconceivable and impossible ; no term of æsthetics can ever represent more than the idea of a phase of the perpetual becoming, a temporary relation in comparative evolution.   Beauty-in-itself is only the name of a sensation, or complex of sensation, mistaken for objectivity — much as sound and light and color were once imagined to be realities.

Yet what is it that attracts ? — what is the meaning of the resistless emotion which we call the Sense of Beauty ?

Like the sensing of light or color or perfume, the recognition of beauty is a recognition of fact. But that fact bears to the feeling evoked no more likeness than the reality of five hundred billions of ether-shiverings per second bears to the sensation of orange.   Still in either case the fact is a manifestation of force.   Representing higher evolution, the phenomenon termed beauty also represents a relatively superior fitness for life, a higher ability to fulfil the conditions of existence ; and it is the non-conscious perception of this representation that makes the fascination.   The longing aroused is not for any mere abstraction, but for greater completeness of faculty as means to the natural end.   To the dead within each man, beauty signifies the presence of what they need most, — Power.   They know, in despite of Lethe, that when they lived in comely bodies life was usually made easy and happy for them, and that when prisoned in feeble or in ugly bodies, they found life miserable or difficult.   They want to live many times again in sound young bodies, — in shapes that assure force, health, joy, quickness to win and energy to keep the best prizes of life's contest.   They want, if possible, conditions better than any of the past, but in no event conditions worse.

III

And so the Riddle resolves itself as Memory, — immeasurable Memory of all bodily fitness for the ends of life: a Composite glorified, doubtless, by some equally measureless inherited sense of all the vanished joys ever associated with such fitness.

Infinite, may we not term it — this Composite? Aye, but not merely because the multitudes of dead memories that make it are unspeakable. Equally unspeakable the width and the depth of the range of them throughout the enormity of Time. . . . O lover, how slender the beautiful witch, — the ghost within the ghost of you! Yet the depth of that ghost is the depth of the Nebulous Zone bespanning Night, — the luminous Shadow that Egypt figured of old as Mother of the Sun and the Gods, curving her long white woman's-body over the world. As a vapor of phosphorus, or wake of a ship in the night, — only so with naked eye can we behold it. But pierced by vision telescopic, it is revealed as the further side of the Ring of the Cosmos, — dim belt of millions of suns seemingly massed together like the cells of a living body, yet so seeming only by reason of their frightful remoteness. Even thus really separated each from each in the awfulness of the Night of Time, — by silent profundities of centuries, — by interspaces of thousands and of myriads of years, — though collectively shaping to love's desire but one dim soft sweet phantom, — are those million-swarming memories that make for youth its luminous dream of beauty.

Sadness in Beauty

Sadness in Beauty

THE poet who sang that beautiful things bring sadness, named as beautiful things music and sunset and night, clear skies and transparent waters. Their sadness he sought to explain by vague soul-memories of Paradise. Very old-fashioned this explanation; but it contains a shadowing of truth. For the mysterious sadness associated with the sense of beauty is certainly not of this existence, but of countless anterior lives, — and therefore indeed a sadness of reminiscence.

Elsewhere I try to explain why certain qualities of music, and certain aspects of sunset produce sadness, and even more than sadness. As for impressions of night, however, I doubt if the emotion that night evokes in this nineteenth century can be classed with the sadness that beauty brings. A wonderful night, — a tropical night, for instance, lucent and lukewarm, with a new moon in it, curved and yellow like a ripe banana, — may inspire, among other minor feelings something of tenderness ; but the great dominant emotion evoked by the splendor of the vision is not sadness.   Breaking open the heavens to their highest, night widens modern thought over the bounds of life and death by the spectacle of that Infinite whose veil is day.   Night also forces remembrance of the mystery of our tether, — the viewless force that holds us down to this wretched little ball of a world.   And the result is cosmic emotion — vaster than any sense of the sublime, — drowning all other emotion, — but nowise akin to the sadness that beauty causes. Anciently the emotion of night must have been incomparably less voluminous.   Men who believed the sky to be a solid vault, never could have felt, as we feel it, the stupendous pomp of darkness.   And our ever-growing admiration of those awful astral questions in the Book of Job, is mainly due to the fact that, with the progress of science, they continue to make larger and larger appeal to forms of thought and feeling which never could have entered into the mind of Job.

But the sadness excited by the beauty of a perfect day, or by the charm of nature in her brightest moods, is a fact of another kind, and needs a different explanation. Inherited the feeling must be, — but through what cumulation of ancestral pain ? Why should the tenderness of an unclouded sky, the soft green sleep of summered valleys, the murmurous peace of sun-flecked shadows, inspire us with sadness ? Why should any inherited emotion following an æsthetic perception be melancholy rather than joyous ? . . . Of course I do not refer to the sense of vastness or permanence or power aroused by the sight of the sea, or by any vision of sea-like space, or by the majesty of colossal ranges. That is the feeling of the sublime, — always related to fear. Æsthetic sadness is related rather to desire.

" All beautiful things bring sadness," is a statement as near to truth as most general statements ; but the sadness and its evolutional history must vary according to circumstances. The melancholy awakened by the sight of a beautiful face cannot be identical with that awakened by the sight of a landscape, by the hearing of music, or by the reading of a poem. Yet there should be some one emotional element common to æsthetic sadness, — one general kind of feeling

which would help us to solve the riddle of the
melancholy inspired by the sight of beauty in
Nature.   Such a common element, I believe, is
inherited longing, — inherited dim sense of loss,
shadowed and qualified variously by interrelated
feelings.   Different forms of this inheritance
would be awakened by different impressions of
the beautiful.   In the case of human beauty, the
æsthetic recognition might be toned or shadowed
by immemorial inheritance of pain — pain of
longing, and pain of separation from numberless
forgotten beloved.   In the case of a color, a
melody, an effect of sunshine or of moonlight,
the sense-impressions appealing to æsthetic feeling
might equally appeal to various ancestral memories of pain.   The melancholy given by the sight
of a beautiful landscape is certainly a melancholy
of longing, — a sadness massive as vague, because
made by the experience of millions of our dead.

" The æsthetic feeling for nature in its purity,"
declares Sully, " is a modern growth . . . the feeling for nature's wild solitudes is hardly older than
Rousseau."   Perhaps to many this will seem rather
a strong statement in regard to the races of the
West ; — it is not true of the races of the Far East,
whose art and poetry yield ancient proof to the

contrary. But no evolutionist would deny that
the æsthetic love of nature has been developed
through civilization, and that many abstract sen-
timents now involved with it are of very recent
origin. Much of the sadness made in us by the
sight of a beautiful landscape would therefore be
of comparatively modern growth, though less
modern than some of the higher qualities of
æsthetic pleasure which accompany the emotion.
I surmise it to be mainly the inherited pain of
that separation from Nature which began with the
building of walled cities. Possibly there is blended
with it something of incomparably older sorrow
— such as the immemorial mourning of man
for the death of summer ; but this, and other
feelings inherited from ages of wandering, would
revive more especially in the great vague melancholy that autumn brings into what we still call
our souls.

Ever as the world increasing its wisdom in-
creases its sorrow, our dwellers in cities built up
to heaven more and more regret the joys of humanity's childhood, — the ancient freedom of
forest and peak and plain, the brightness of
mountain water, the cool keen sweetness of the

sea's breath and the thunder-roll of its eternal
epic. And all this regret of civilization for Nature irretrievably forsaken, may somehow revive
in that great soft dim sadness which the beauty
of a landscape makes us feel.

In one sense we are certainly wrong when we
say that the loveliness of a scene brings tears to
the eyes. It cannot be the loveliness of the scene;
— it is the longing of generations quickening
in the hearts of us. The beauty we speak of
has no real existence : the emotion of the dead
alone makes it seem to be, — the emotion of
those long-buried millions of men and women
who loved Nature for reasons very much simpler
and older than any æsthetic emotion is. To the
windows of the house of life their phantoms
crowd, — like prisoners toward some vision of
bright skies and flying birds, free hills and glim-
mering streams, beyond the iron of their bars.
They behold their desire of other time, — the
vast light and space of the world, the wind-
swept clearness of azure, the hundred greens of
wold and plain, the spectral promise of summits
far away. They hear the shrilling and the whirr
of happy winged things, the chorus of cicada and
bird, the lisping and laughing of water, the under-

tone of leafage astir. They know the smell of
the season — all sharp sweet odors of sap, scents
of flower and fruitage. They feel the quickening of the living air, — the thrilling of the great
Blue Ghost.

But all this comes to them, filtered through the
bars and veils of their rebirth, only as dreams of
home to hopeless exile, — of child-bliss to deso-
late age, — of remembered vision to the blind!

Parfum de Jeunesse

Parfum de Jeunesse

"I REMEMBER," — said an old friend, telling me the romance of his youth, — "that I could always find her cloak in the cloak-room without a light, when it was time to take her home. I used to know it in the dark, because it had the smell of sweet new milk. . . ."

Which set me somehow to thinking of English dawns, the scent of hayfields, the fragrance of hawthorn days; — and cluster after cluster of memories lighted up in succession through a great arc of remembrance that flashed over half a lifetime even before my friend's last words had ceased to sound in my ears. And then recollection smouldered into revery, — a revery about the riddle of the odor of youth.

That quality of the *parfum de jeunesse* which my friend described is not uncommon, — though I fancy that it belongs to Northern rather than to

Southern races. It signifies perfect health and splendid vigor. But there are other and more delicate varieties of the attraction. Sometimes it may cause you to think of precious gums or spices from the uttermost tropics; sometimes it is a thin, thin sweetness, — like a ghost of musk. It is not personal (though physical personality certainly has an odor): it is the fragrance of a season, — of the springtime of life. But even as the fragrance of spring, though everywhere a passing delight, varies with country and climate, so varies the fragrance of youth.

Whether it be of one sex more than of another were difficult to say. We notice it chiefly in girls and in children with long hair, probably because it dwells especially in the hair. But it is always independent of artifice as the sweetness of the wild violet is. It belongs to the youth of the savage not less than to the youth of the civilized, — to the adolescence of the peasant not less than to that of the prince. It is not found in the sickly and the feeble, but only in perfect joyous health. Perhaps, like beauty, it may have some vague general relation to conditions ethical. Individual odors assuredly have, — as the discrimination of the dog gives witness.

Evolutionists have suggested that the pleasure we find in the perfume of a flower may be an emotional reflection from æons enormously remote, when such odor announced, to forms of ancestral life far lower than human, the presence of savory food. To what organic memory of association might be due, upon the same hypothesis, our pleasure in the perfume of youth?

Perhaps there were ages in which that perfume had significances more definite and special than any which we can now attach to it. Like the pleasure yielded by the fragrance of flowers, the pleasure given by the healthy fragrance of a young body may be, partly at least, a survival from some era in which odorous impressions made direct appeal to the simplest of life-serving impulses. Long dissociated from such possible primitive relation, odor of blossom and odor of youth alike have now become for us excitants of the higher emotional life, — of vague but voluminous and supremely delicate æsthetic feeling.

Like the feeling awakened by beauty, the pleasure of odor is a pleasure of remembrance, — is the magical appeal of a sensation to countless memories of countless lives. And even as the scent of a blossom evokes the ghosts of feelings experienced in millions of millions of unrecorded springs, — so the fragrance of youth bestirs within us the spectral survival of sensations associated with every vernal cycle of all the human existence that has vanished behind us.

And this fragrance of fresh being likewise makes invocation to ideal sentiment, — to parental scarcely less than to amorous tenderness, — because conjoined through immeasurable time with the charm and the beauty of childhood. Out of night and death is summoned by its necromancy more than a shadowy thrill from the rapture of perished passion, — more than a phantom-reflex from the delight of countless bridals; — even something also of the ecstasy of pressing lips of caress to the silky head of the first-born, — faint refluence from the forgotten joy of myriad millions of buried mothers.

Azure Psychology

Azure Psychology

I

LEAST common of the colors given by nature to bird, insect, and blossom is bright
pure blue. Blue flowers are believed to
proclaim for the plant that bears them a longer
history of unchecked development than flowers of
any other primary color suggest; and the high
cost of the tint is perhaps hinted by the inability
of the horticulturist to produce blue roses or blue
chrysanthemums. Vivid blue appears in the
plumage of some wonderful birds, and on the
wings of certain amazing butterflies — especially
tropical butterflies; — but usually under conditions that intimate a prodigious period of evolutional specialization. Altogether it would seem
that blue was the latest pure color developed in
the evolution of flower and scale and feather; and
there is reason to believe that the power of perceiving blue was not acquired until after the power

of distinguishing red and green and yellow had already been gained.

Whether the hypothesis be true or false, it is certainly noteworthy that, of the primary colors, blue alone has remained, up to the present time, a color pleasurable in its purest intensity to the vision of highly civilized races. Bright red, bright green, bright orange, yellow, or violet, can be used but sparingly in our nineteenth-century attire and decoration. They have become offensive in their spectral purity because of the violence of the sensations that they give; — they remain grateful only to the rudimentary æsthetic feeling of children, of the totally uncultivated, or of savages. What modern beauty clothes herself in scarlet, or robes herself in fairy green? We cannot paint our chambers violet or saffron — the mere idea jars upon our nerves. But the color of heaven has not ceased to delight us. Sky-blue can still be worn by our fairest; and the luminous charm of azure ceilings and azure wall-surfaces — under certain conditions of lighting and dimension — is still recognized.

"Nevertheless," some one may say, "we do not paint the *outside* of a building skyblue; and a skyblue façade would be even more disagreeable than an orange or a crimson façade." This is true,— but not because the effect of the color upon large surfaces is necessarily displeasing. It is true only because vivid blue, unlike other bright colors, is never associated in our experience of nature with large and opaque *solidity*. When mountains become blue for us, they also become ghostly and semi-transparent. Upon a housefront the color must appear monstrous, because giving the notion of the unnatural, — of a huge blue dead solidity tangibly proximate. But a blue ceiling, a blue vault, blue walls of corridors, may suggest the true relation of the color to depth and transparency, and make for us a grateful illusion of space and summer-light. Yellow, on the other hand, is a color well adapted to façades, because associated in memory with the beautiful effect of dying sunlight over pale broad surfaces.

But although yellow remains, after blue, the most agreeable of the primary colors, it cannot often be used for artistic purposes, like blue, in all its luminous strength. Pale tones of yellow, — especially creamy tones, — are capable of an immense variety of artistic employment; but this is not true of the brilliant and burning yellow. Only blue is always agreeable in its most vivid purity — providing that it be not used in massive displays so as to suggest the anomaly of blue hardness and blue opacity.[1]

In Japan, which may still be called the land of perfect good taste in chromatics — notwithstanding the temporary apparition of some discords due to Western influence, — almost any ordinary street-vista tells the story of the race-experience with color. The general tone of the vista is given by bluish greys above and dark blues below, sharply relieved by numerous small details of white and cool yellow. In this perspective the bluish-greys represent the tiling of roofs and awnings ; the dark blues, shop-draperies ; the bright whites, narrow strips of plastered surface ; the pale yellows, mostly smooth naked wood, and glimpses of rush-mattings. The broader stretches of color are furthermore relieved and softened by the sprinkling of countless ideographs over draperies and shop-signs — black, (and sometimes red) against white ; white or

[1] Blue jewels, blue eyes, blue flowers delight us; but in these the color accompanies either transparency or visible softness. It is perhaps because of the incongruity between hard opacity and blue that the sight of a book in sky-blue binding is unendurable. I can imagine nothing more atrocious.

gold on blue.   Strong yellows, greens, oranges,
purples are invisible.   In dress also greys and
cool blues rule: when you do happen to see
robes or *hakama* all of one brilliant color, —
worn by children or young girls, — that color is
either a sky-blue, or a violet with only just enough
red in it to kindle the azure, — a rainbow-violet
of exquisite luminosity.[1]

II

But I wish to speak neither of the æsthetic
value of blue in relation to arts and industries,
nor of the optical significance of blue as the pro-
duct of six hundred and fifty billion oscillations
of the luminous ether per second.   I only want
to say something about the psychology of the
color, — about its subjective evolutional history.
Certainly the same apparition of blue will bestir

[1] This essay was written several years ago.   During
1897 I noticed for the first time since my arrival in Japan
a sprinkling of dark greens and light-yellows in the fashions
of the season; but the general tone of costume was little
affected by these exceptions to older taste.   The light-
yellow appeared only in some girdles of children.

in different minds different degrees of feeling, and
will set in motion, through memory-revival of
unlike experiences, totally dissimilar operations of
fancy.   But independently of such psychological
variation — mainly personal and superficial, —
there can be no doubt that the color evokes in
the *general* mind one common quality of pleasurable feeling, — a vivacious thrill, — a tone of
emotional activity unmistakably related to the
higher zones of sentiency and of imagination.

In my own case the sight of vivid blue has
always been accompanied by an emotion of vague
delight — more or less strong according to the
luminous intensity of the color.   And in one
experience of travel, — sailing to the American
tropics, — this feeling rose into ecstasy.   It was
when I beheld for the first time the grandest
vision of blue in this world, — the glory of the
Gulf-Stream : a magical splendor that made me
doubt my senses, — a flaming azure that looked
as if a million summer skies had been condensed
into pure fluid color for the making of it.   The
captain of the ship leaned over the rail with me ;
and we both watched the marvellous sea for a
long time in silence.   Then he said : —

" Fifteen years ago I took my wife with me on this trip — just after we were married, it was; — and she wondered at the water. She asked me to get her a silk dress of the very same color. I tried in ever so many places; but I never could get just what she wanted till a chance took me to Canton. I went round the Chinese silk-shops day after day, looking for that color. It was n't easy to find; but I did get it at last. Was n't she glad, though, when I brought it home to her! . . . She 's got it yet. . . ."

Still, at times, in sleep, I sail southward again over the wonder of that dazzling surging azure; — then the dream shifts suddenly across the world, and I am wandering with the Captain through close dim queer Chinese streets, — vainly seeking a silk of the Blue of the Gulf-Stream. And it was this memory of tropic days that first impelled me to think about the reason of the delight inspired by the color.

III

Possibly the wave of pleasurable emotion ex·
cited by a glorious vision of blue is not more com·
plex than the feeling aroused by any massive
display of any other pure color; — but it is
higher in the quality of its complexity. For the
ideational elements that blend in the volume of it
include not a few of the noblest, — not a few of
those which also enter into the making of Cosmic
Emotion.

Being the seeming color of the ghost of our
planet, — of the breath of the life of the world, —
blue is likewise the color apparent of the enormity
of day and the abyss of the night. So the sensation of it makes appeal to the ideas of Altitude,
of Vastness, and of Profundity; —

Also to the idea of Space in Time; for blue is
the tint of distance and of vagueness; —

Also to the idea of Motion; for blue is the
color of Vanishing and of Apparition. Peak and
vale, bay and promontory, turn blue as we leave
them; and out of blue they grow and define
again as we glide homeward.

And therefore in the volume of feeling awakened in us by the sensation of blue, there should
be something of the emotion associated with experience of change, — with countless ancestral
sorrows of parting.   But if there indeed be any
such dim survival, it is utterly whelmed and lost
in that all-radiant emotional inheritance related
to Summer and Warmth, — to the joy of past
humanity in the light of cloudless days.

Still more significant is the fact that although
blue is a sacred color, the dominant tones of the
feeling it evokes are gladness and tenderness.
Blue speaks to us of the dead and of the gods,
but never of their awfulness.

Now when we reflect that blue is the color of
the idea of the divine, the color pantheistic, the
color ethical, — thrilling most deeply into those
structures of thought to which belong our senti-
ments of reverence and justice, of duty and of
aspiration, — we may wonder why the emotion it
calls up should be supremely gladsome.   Is it because that sensuous race-experience of blue skies,
— that measureless joy of the dead in light and
warmth, which has been transmitted to each of us
in organic memory, — is vastly older than the

religious idea, and therefore voluminous enough to drown any ethical feeling indirectly related to the color-sensation ? Partly so, no doubt ; — but I will venture another, and a very simple explanation : —

All moral pulsations in the wave of inherited feeling which responds to the impression of blue, belong only to the beautiful and tender aspects of faith.

And thus much having been ventured, I may presume a little further.

I imagine that for many of us one of the most powerful elements in this billow of pleasurable feeling evoked by the vision of blue, *is* spiritual, in the fullest ethical meaning of the word ; — that under the fleeting surface-plexus of personal emotion empirically associated with the color, pulses like a tide the transmitted religious emotion of unnumbered ages ; — and that, quickening and vivifying all inherited sense of blue as beauty, is the inherited lucent rapture of blue as the splendor mystical, — as the color of the everlasting Peace. Something of all human longing for all the Paradises ever imagined, — of all pre-existent trust in the promise of reunion after death, — of all expired dreams of unending youth and bliss, — may be revived for us, more or less faintly, in this thrill of the delight of azure. Even as through the jewel-radiance of the Tropic Stream pass undulations from the vaster deep, — with their sobbings and whisperings, their fugitive drift and foam, — so, through the emotion evoked by the vision of luminous blue, there may somehow quiver back to us out of the Infinite — (multitudinous like the billion ether-shiverings that make the blue sensation of a moment) — something of all the aspirations of the ancient faiths, and the power of the vanished gods, and the passion and the beauty of all the prayer ever uttered by lips of man.

A Serenade

A Serenade

"BROKEN" were too abrupt a word. My sleep was not broken, but suddenly melted and swept away by a flow of music from the night without, — music that filled me with expectant ecstasy by the very first gush of its sweetness: a serenade, — a playing of flutes and mandolines.

The flutes had dove-tones; and they cooed and moaned and purled; — and the mandolines throbbed through the liquid plaint of them, like a beating of hearts. The players I could not see: they were standing in heavy shadows flung into the street by a tropical moon, — shadows of plantain and of tamarind.

Nothing in all the violet gloom moved but that music, and the fire-flies, — great bright slow sparks of orange and of emerald. The warm air held its breath; the plumes of the palms were

16

still; and the haunting circle of the sea, blue even
beneath the moon, lay soundless as a circle of
vapor.

Flutes and mandolines — a Spanish melody —
nothing more.   Yet it seemed as if the night itself were speaking, or, out of the night some passional life long since melted into Nature's mystery,
but continuing to haunt the tepid, odorous, spark-
ling darkness of that strange world, which sleeps
under the sun, and wakens only to the stars.
And its utterance was the ghostly reiteration of
rapture that had been, and never again could be,
— an utterance of infinite tenderness and of immeasurable regret.

Never before had I felt how the simplest of
music could express what no other art is able even
to suggest ; — never before had I known the astonishing possibilities of melody without orna-
ment, without artifice, — yet with a charm as
bewildering, as inapprehensible, as the Greek
perception of the grace supreme.

Now nothing in perfect art can be only volup-
tuous ; and this music, in despite of its caress,
was immeasurably, ineffably sad.   And the exquisite blending of melancholy with passion in a

motive so simple, — one low long cooing motive,
over and over again repeated, like a dove's cry,
— had a *strangeness* of beauty like the musical
thought of a vanished time, — one rare survival,
out of an era more warmly human than our own,
of some lost art of melody.

II

The music hushed, and left me dreaming, and
vainly trying to explain the emotion that it had
made. Of one thing only I felt assured, — that
the mystery was of other existences than mine.

For the living present, I reflected, is the whole
dead past. Our pleasures and our pains alike
are but products of evolution, — vast complexities
of sentiency created by experience of vanished
beings more countless than the sands of a myriad
seas. All personality is recombination; and all
emotions are of the dead. Yet some seem to us
more ghostly than others, — partly because of
their greater relative mystery, partly because of
the immense power of the phantom waves composing them. Among pleasurable forms, the
ghostliest are the emotion of first love, the emo-

tion following the perception of the sublime in
nature — of terrible beauty, — and the emotion
of music. Why should they so be? Probably
because the influences that arouse them thrill
furthest into our forgotten past. Frightful as the
depth of the abyss of Space is the depth of one
thinking life, — measureless even by millions of
ages ; — and who may divine how profoundly in
certain personalities the mystery can be moved.
We only know that the deeper the thrilling, the
heavier the wave responding, and the weirder the
result, — until those profundities are reached of
which a single surge brings instant death, or
makes perpetual ruin of the delicate structures
of thought.

Now any music that makes powerful appeal
to the emotion of love, awakening the passional
latency of the past within us, must inevitably
revive dead pain not less than dead delight. Pain
of the conquest of will by a mystery resistless and
pitiless, the torture of doubt, the pangs of rivalry,
the terror of impermanency, — shadows of these
and many another sorrow have had their part in
the toning of that psychical inheritance which
makes at once love's joy and love's anguish, and
grows forever from birth to birth.

And thus it may happen that a child, innocent
of passion or of real pain, is moved even to tears
by music uttering either. Unknowingly he feels
in that utterance a shadowing of the sorrow of
numberless vanished lives.

III

But it seemed to me that the extraordinary
emotion awakened by that tropical melody needed
an explanation more qualitative than the explanation above attempted. I felt sure that the dead
past to which the music had made appeal must
have been a special past, — that some particular
class or group of emotional memories had been
touched. Yet what class? — what group? For
the time being, I could not even venture a guess.

Long afterwards, however, some chance hap-
pening revived for me with surprising distinctness
the memory of the serenade; — and simultaneously, like a revelation, came the certainty that
the whole spell of the melody — all its sadness
and all its sweetness — had been supremely and
uniquely *feminine*.

— " Assuredly," I reflected, as the new conviction grew upon me, " the primal source of all human tenderness has been the Eternal Feminine. . . . Yet how should melody uttering only the soul of woman have been composed by man, and bestir within man this innominable quickening of emotional reminiscence ? "

The answer shaped itself at once, —

— " *Every mortal man has been many millions of times a woman.*"

Undoubtedly in either sex survives the sum of the feelings and of the memories of both. But some rare experience may appeal at times to the feminine element of personality alone, — to one half only of the phantom-world of Self, — leaving the other hemisphere dormant and unillumed. And such experience had found embodiment in the marvellous melody of the serenade which I had heard.

That tremulous sweetness was never masculine ; that passional sadness never was of man : — unisexual both and inseparably blended into a single miracle of tone-beauty. Echoing far into the mystery of my own past, the enchantment of that tone had startled from their sleep of ages count-

less buried loves, and set the whole delicate swarm
fluttering in some delicious filmy agony of revival,
—set them streaming and palpitating through the
Night of Time,—like those myriads eddying
forever through the gloom of the vision of Dante.

They died with the music and the moon,—but
not utterly. Whenever in dream the memory of
that melody returns, again I feel the long soft
shuddering of the dead,—again I feel the faint
wings spread and thrill, responsive to the cooing
of those spectral flutes, to the throbbing of those
shadowy mandolines. And the elfish ecstasy of
their thronging awakes me; but always with
my wakening the delight passes, and in the
dark the sadness only lingers,—unutterable,—
infinite. . . !

A Red Sunset

A Red Sunset

I

THE most stupendous apparition of red that I ever saw was a tropical sunset in a cloudless sky, — a sunset such as can be witnessed only during exceptional conditions of atmosphere. It began with a flaming of orange from horizon to zenith ; and this quickly deepened to a fervid vermilion, through which the crimson disk glared like the cinder of a burnt-out star. Sea, peak, and palm caught the infernal glow ; and I became conscious of a vague strange horror within myself, — a sense of distress like that which precedes a nightmare. I could not then explain the feeling ; — I only knew that the color had aroused it.

But how aroused it ? — I later asked myself. Common theories about the ugly sensation of bright red could not explain for me the weirdness

of that experience.   As for the sanguine associations of the color, they could interpret little in
my case ; for the sight of blood had never affected
my nerves in the least.   I thought that the theory
of psychical inheritance might furnish some explanation ; — but how could it meet the fact that a
color, which the adult finds insufferable, continues
to delight the child ?

All ruddy tones, however, are not unpleasant
to refined sensibility : some are quite the reverse,
— as, for example, the various tender colors called
pink or rose.   These appeal to very agreeable
kinds of sensuous experience : they suggest delicacy and softness ; they awaken qualities of
feeling totally different from those excited by
vermilion or scarlet.   Pink, being the tint of the
blossoming of flowers and the blossoming of
youth, — of the ripeness of fruit and the ripeness of flesh, is ever associated with impressions
of fragrance and sweetness, and with memories
of beautiful lips and cheeks.

No : it is only the pure brilliant red, the fervid
red, that arouses sinister feeling.   Experience with
this color seems to have been the same even in
societies evolved under conditions utterly unlike
those of our own history, — Japan being a signifi-

cant example. The more refined and humane a
civilization becomes, the less are displays of the
color tolerated in its cultivated circles. But how
are we to account for that pleasure which bright
red still gives to the children of the people who
detest it ?

II

Many sensations which delighted us as children,
prove to us either insipid or offensive in adult life.
Why ? Because there have grown up with our
growth feelings which, though now related to
them, were dormant during childhood ; ideas
now associated with them, but undeveloped during childhood : and experiences connected with
them, never imagined in childhood.

For the mind, at our birth, is even less developed than the body ; and its full ripening demands
very much more time than is needed for the perfect bodily growth. Both by his faults and by
his virtues the child resembles the savage, because
the instincts and the emotions of the primitive man
are the first to mature within him ; — and they
are the first to mature in the individual because
they were the first evolved in the history of the

race, being the most necessary to self-maintenance.
That in later adult life they take a very inferior
place is because the nobler mental and moral
qualities — comparatively recent products of social
discipline and civilized habit — have at last gained
massiveness enough to dominate them under
normal conditions ; — have become like powerful
new senses upon which the primitive emotional
nature learns to depend for guidance.

All emotions are inheritances ; but the higher,
because in evolutional order the latest, develop
only with the complete unfolding of the brain.
Some, ethically considered the very loftiest, are
said to develop only in old age, — to which they
impart a particular charm. Other faculties also
of a high order, chiefly æsthetic, would seem in
the average of cases to mature in middle life.
And to this period of personal evolution probably
belongs the finer sense of beauty in color, — a
much simpler faculty than the ethical sense,
though possibly related to it in ways unsuspected.

Vivid colors appeal to the rudimentary æsthetic
sense of our children, as they do to the æsthetic
sense of savages ; but the civilized adult dislikes most of the very vivid colors : they exasper-
ate his nerves like an excessive crash of brass and

drums during a cheap orchestral performance.
Cultured vision especially shrinks from a strong
blaze of red. Only the child delights in vermilion and scarlet. Growing up he gradually learns
to think of what we call "loud red" as vulgar,
and to dislike it much more than did his less delicate ancestors of the preceding century. Educa-
tion helps him to explain why he thinks it vulgar,
but not to explain why he *feels* it to be unpleasant, — independently of the question whether it
tires his eyes.

III

And now I come back to the subject of that
tropical sunset.

Even in the common æsthetic emotion excited
by the spectacle of any fine sunset, there are elements of feeling ancient as the race, — dim melancholy, dim fear, inherited from ages when the
dying of the day was ever watched with sadness
and foreboding. After that mighty glow, the
hours of primeval horror, — the fear of blackness, the fear of nocturnal foes, the fear of
ghosts. These, and other weird feelings, — independently of the physical depression following

the withdrawal of sunlight, — would by inheritance become emotionally related to visions of
sundown; and the primitive horror would at last
be evolutionally transmuted to one elemental tone
of the modern sublime.   But the spectacle of a
vast *crimson* sunset would awaken feelings less
vague than the sense of the sublime, — feelings of a definitely sinister kind.   The very
color itself would make appeal to special kinds
of inherited feelings, simply because of its relation to awful spectacles, — the glare of the vol-
cano-summit, the furious vermilion of lava, the
raging of forest-fires, the overglow of cities kind-
ling in the track of war, the smouldering of ruin,
the blazing of funeral-pyres.   And in this lurid
race-memory of fire as destroyer, — as the " ravening ghost " of Northern fancy, — there would
mingle a vague distress evolved through ancestral experience of *crimson heat in relation to
pain*, — an organic horror.   And the like tremendous color in celestial phenomena would revive also inherited terror related of old to ideas
of the portentous and of the wrath of gods.

Probably the largest element of the unpleasant
feeling aroused in man by this angry color has

been made by the experience of the race with fire. But in even the most vivid red there is always some suggestion of passion, and of the tint of blood. Inherited emotion related to the sight of death must be counted among the elements of the sinister feeling that the hue excites. Doubtless for the man, as for the bull, the emotional wave called up by displays of violent red, is mostly the creation of impressions and of tendencies accumulated through all the immense life of the race ; and, as in the old story of Thomas the Rhymer, we can say of our only real Fairyland, our ghostly past, —

. . . " *A' the blude that's shed on earth*
Rins through the springs o' that Countrie."

But those very associations that make burning red unbearable to modern nerves must have already been enormously old when it first became the color of pomp and luxury. How then should such associations affect us unpleasantly now ?

I would answer that the emotional suggestions of the color continued to be pleasurable for the adult, as they still are for the child, only while they remained more vague and much less voluminous than at present. Becoming intensified in

17

the modern brain, they gradually ceased to yield
pleasure, — somewhat as warmth increased to the
degree of heat ceases to be pleasurable.   Still later
they became painful ; and their actual painfulness
exposes the fundamentally savage nature of those
sensations of splendor and power which the color
once called into play.   And the intensification
of the feeling evoked by red has not been due
merely to later accumulation of inherited impressions, but also to the growth and development of
emotions essentially antithetical to ideas of violence
and pain, and yet inseparable from them.   The
moral sensibility of an eia that has condemned
not a few of the amusements of our forebears to
the limbo of old barbarities, — the humanity of
an age that refuses to believe in a hell of literal
fire, that prohibits every brutal sport, that com-
pels kindness to animals, — is offended by the
cruel suggestiveness of the color.   But within the
slowly-unfolding brain of the child, this modern
sensibility is not evolved ; — and until it has been
evolved, with the aid of experience and of educa-
tion, the feeling aroused by such a color as vivid
scarlet will naturally continue to be pleasurable
rather than painful.

IV

While thus trying to explain why a color dignified as imperial in other centuries should have become offensive in our own, I found myself wondering whether most of our actual refinements might not in like manner become the vulgarities of a future age. Our standards of taste and our ideals of beauty can have only a value relative to conditions which are constantly changing. Real and ideal alike are transitory, — mere apparitional undulations in the flux of the perpetual Becoming. Perhaps the finest ethical or æsthetical sentiment of to-day will manifest itself in another era only as some extraordinary psychological atavism, — some rare individual reversion to the conditions of a barbarous past.

What in the meantime would be the fate of sensations that are even now becoming intolerable? Any faculty, mental or physical, however previously developed by evolutional necessities, would have a tendency to dwindle and disappear from the moment that it ceased to be either useful or pleasurable. Continuance of the power to perceive red would depend upon the possible

future usefulness of that power to the race.   Not
without suggestiveness in this connection may be
the fact that it represents the lowest rate of those
ether-oscillations which produce color.   Perhaps
our increasing dislike to it indicates that power to
distinguish it will eventually pass away — pass
away in a sort of Daltonism at the inferior end
of the color-scale.   Such visual loss would probably be more than compensated by superior coincident specializations of retinal sensibility.   A
more highly organized generation might enjoy
wonders of color now unimaginable, and yet
never be able to perceive red, — not, at least, that
red whose sensation is the spectral smouldering
of the agonies and the furies of our evolutional
past, — the haunting of a horror innominable,
immeasurable, — enormous phantom-menace of
expired human pain.

Frisson

Frisson

SOME there may be who have never felt the thrill of a human touch; but surely these are few! Most of us in early childhood discover strange differences in physical contact; — we find that some caresses soothe, while others irritate; and we form in consequence various unreasoning likes and antipathies. With the ripening of youth we seem to feel these distinctions more and more keenly, — until the fateful day in which we learn that a certain feminine touch communicates an unspeakable shiver of delight, — exercises a witchcraft that we try to account for by theories of the occult and the supernatural. Age may smile at these magical fancies of youth; and nevertheless, in spite of much science, the imagination of the lover is probably nearer to truth than is the wisdom of the disillusioned.

We seldom permit ourselves in mature life to think very seriously about such experiences. We do not deny them; but we incline to regard them as nervous idiosyncrasies. We scarcely notice that even in the daily act of shaking hands with persons of either sex, sensations may be received which no physiology can explain.

I remember the touch of many hands, — the quality of each clasp, the sense of physical sympathy or repulsion aroused. Thousands I have indeed forgotten, — probably because their contact told me nothing in particular; but the strong experiences I fully recollect. I found that their agreeable or disagreeable character was often quite independent of the moral relation: but in the most extraordinary case that I can recall — (a strangely fascinating personality with the strangest of careers as poet, soldier, and refugee) — the moral and the physical charm were equally powerful and equally rare. "Whenever I shake hands with that man," said to me one of many who had yielded to his spell, "I feel a warm shock go all through me, like a glow of summer." Even at this moment when I think of that dead hand, I can feel it reached out to me over the space of twenty years and of many

a thousand miles. Yet it was a hand that had
killed. . . .

These, with other memories and reflections,
came to me just after reading a criticism on Mr.
Bain's evolutional interpretation of the thrill of
pleasure sometimes given by the touch of the
human skin. The critic asked why a satin
cushion kept at a temperature of about 98°
would not give the same thrill; and the question
seemed to me unfair because, in the very passage
criticised, Mr. Bain had sufficiently suggested the
reason. Taking him to have meant — as he must
have meant, — not that the thrill is given by any
kind of warmth and softness, but only by the
peculiar warmth and softness of the human skin,
his interpretation can scarcely be contested by a
sarcasm. A satin cushion at a temperature of
about 98° could not give the same sensation as
that given by the touch of the human skin for
reasons even much more simple than Mr. Bain
implied, — since it is totally different from the
human skin in substance, in texture, and in the
all-important fact that it is not alive, but dead.
Of course warmth and softness in themselves are
not enough to produce the thrill of pleasure con-

sidered by Mr. Bain : under easily imaginable circumstances they may produce something of the
reverse.   Smoothness has quite as much to do
with the pleasure of touch as either softness or
warmth can have; yet a moist or a very dry
smoothness may be disagreeable.   Again, cool
smoothness in the human skin is perhaps even
more agreeable than warm smoothness; yet there
is a cool smoothness common to many lower
forms of life which causes a shudder.   Whatever be
those qualities making pleasurable the touch of a
hand, for example, they are probably very many
in combination, and they are certainly peculiar to
the *living* touch.   No possible artificial combination of warmth and smoothness and softnesss
combined could excite the same quality of pleasure
that certain human touches give,— although, as
other psychologists than Mr. Bain have observed,
it may give rise to a fainter kind of agreeable
feeling.

A special sensation can be explained only by
special conditions.   Some philosophers would explain the conditions producing this pleasurable
thrill, or *frisson*, as mainly subjective ; others, as
mainly objective.   Is it not most likely that either
view contains truth ;— that the physical cause

must be sought in some quality, definable or indefinable, attaching to a particular touch; and that
the cause of the coincident emotional phenomena
should be looked for in the experience, not of the
individual, but of the race?

Remembering that there can be no two tangible things exactly alike, — no two blades of
grass, or drops of water, or grains of sand, — it
ought not to seem incredible that the touch of
one person should have power to impart a sensation different from any sensation producible by
the touch of any other person. That such difference could neither be estimated nor qualified
would not necessarily imply unimportance or
even feebleness. Among the voices of the thousands of millions of human beings in this world,
there are no two precisely the same; — yet how
much to the ear and to the heart of wife or mother,
child or lover, may signify the unspeakably fine
difference by which each of a billion voices varies
from every other! Not even in thought, much
less in words, can such distinction be specified;
but who is unfamiliar with the fact and with its
immense relative importance?

That any two human skins should be abso-

lutely alike is not possible. There are individual
variations perceptible even to the naked eye, —
for has not Mr. Galton taught us that the visible
finger-marks of no two persons are the same?
But in addition to differences visible — whether
to the naked eye, or only under the microscope,
there must be other differences of quality de-
pending upon constitutional vigor, upon nervous and glandular activities, upon relative
chemical composition of tissue. Whether touch
be a sense delicate enough to discern such differences, would be, of course, a question for
psycho-physics to decide, — and a question not
simply of magnitudes, but of qualities of sensation. Perhaps it is not yet even legitimate to
suppose that, just as by ear we can distinguish
the qualitative differences of a million voices, so
by touch we might be able to distinguish qualitative differences of surface scarcely less delicate.
Yet it is worth while here to remark that the
tingle or shiver of pleasure excited in us by certain qualities of voice, very much resembles the
thrill given sometimes by the touch of a hand.
Is it not possible that there may be recognized, in
the particular quality of a living skin, something
not less uniquely attractive than the indeter-

minable charm of what we call a bewitching voice?

Perhaps it is not impossible. But in the character of the *frisson* itself there is a hint that the charm of the touch provoking it may be due to something much more deeply vital than any physical combination of smoothness, warmth and softness, — to something, as Mr. Bain has suggested, electric or magnetic. Human electricity is no fiction: every living body, — even a plant, — is to some degree electrical; and the electric conditions of no two organisms would be exactly the same. Can the thrill be partly accounted for by some individual peculiarity of these conditions? May there not be electrical differences of touch appreciable by delicate nervous systems, — differences subtle as those infinitesimal variations of timbre by which every voice of a million voices is known from every other?

Such a theory might be offered in explanation of the fact that the slightest touch of a particular woman, for example, will cause a shock of pleasure to men whom the caresses of other and fairer women would leave indifferent. But it could not serve to explain why the same contact should

produce no effect upon some persons, while caus-
ing ecstasy in others.   No purely physical theory
can interpret all the mystery of the *frisson*.   A
deeper explanation is needed; — and I imagine
that one is suggested by the phenomenon of
" love *at first sight*."

The power of a woman to inspire love at first
sight does not depend upon some attraction
visible to the common eye. It depends partly
upon something objective which only certain
eyes can see; and it depends partly upon something which no mortal can see, — *the psychical
composition of the subject of the passion*.   Nobody can pretend to explain in detail the whole
enigma of first love.   But a general explanation
is suggested by evolutional philosophy, — namely,
that the attraction depends upon an inherited individual susceptibility to special qualities of feminine influence, and subjectively represents a kind
of superindividual recognition, — a sudden wakening of that inherited composite memory which
is more commonly called " passional affinity."
Certainly if first love be evolutionally explicable,
it means the perception by the lover of something differentiating the beloved from all other
women, — something corresponding to an in-

herited ideal within himself, previously latent, but suddenly lighted and defined by result of that visual impression.

And like sight, though perhaps less deeply, do other of our senses reach into the buried past. A single strain of melody, the sweetness of a single voice — what thrill immeasurable will either make in the fathomless sleep of ancestral memory! Again, who does not know that speechless delight bestirred in us on rare bright days by something odorous in the atmosphere, — enchanting, but indefinable? The first breath of spring, the blowing of a mountain breeze, a south wind from the sea may bring this emotion, — an emotion overwhelming, yet nameless as its cause, — an ecstasy formless and transparent as the air. Whatever be the odor, diluted to very ghostliness, that arouses this delight, the delight itself is too weirdly voluminous to be explained by any memory-revival of merely individual experience. More probably it is older even than human life, — reaches deeper into the infinite blind depth of dead pleasure and pain.

Out of that ghostly abyss also must come the thrill responding within us to a living touch, — touch electrical of man, questioning the heart, —

touch magical of woman, invoking memory of caresses given by countless delicate and loving hands long crumbled into dust. Doubt it not! — the touch that makes a thrill within you is a touch that you have felt before, — sense-echo of forgotten intimacies in many unremembered lives!

Vespertina Cognitio

Vespertina Cognitio

1

I DOUBT if there be any other form of terror
that even approaches the fear of the supernatural, — and more especially the fear of
the supernatural in dreams. Children know this
fear both by night and by day; but the adult
is not likely to suffer from it except in slumber,
or under the most abnormal conditions of mind
produced by illness. Reason, in our healthy waking hours, keeps the play of ideas far above those
deep-lying regions of inherited emotion where
dwell the primitive forms of terror. But even as
known to the adult in dreams only, there is no
waking fear comparable to this fear, — none so
deep and yet so vague, — none so unutterable.
The indefiniteness of the horror renders verbal
expression of it impossible; yet the suffering is
so intense that, if prolonged beyond a certain
term of seconds, it will kill. And the reason

is that such fear is not of the individual life: it
is infinitely more massive than any personal
experience could account for ; — it is prenatal,
ancestral fear.   Dim it necessarily is, because
compounded of countless blurred millions of inherited fears.   But for the same reason, its depth
is abysmal.

The training of the mind under civilization has
been directed toward the conquest of fear in general, and — excepting that ethical quality of the
feeling which belongs to religion — of the supernatural in particular.   Potentially in most of us
this fear exists ; but its sources are well-guarded ;
and outside of sleep it can scarcely perturb any
vigorous mind except in the presence of facts so
foreign to all relative experience that the imagination is clutched before the reason can grapple
with the surprise.

Once only, after the period of childhood, I
knew this emotion in a strong form.   It was remarkable as representing the vivid projection of a
dream-fear into waking consciousness ; and the
experience was peculiarly tropical.   In tropical
countries, owing to atmospheric conditions, the
oppression of dreams is a more serious suffering
than with us, and is perhaps most common dur-

ing the siesta. All who can afford it pass their
nights in the country; but for obvious reasons
the majority of colonists must be content to take
their siesta, and its consequences, in town.

The West-Indian siesta does not refresh like
that dreamless midday nap which we enjoy in
Northern summers. It is a stupefaction rather
than a sleep, — beginning with a miserable feeling
of weight at the base of the brain: it is a helpless
surrender of the whole mental and physical being
to the overpressure of light and heat. Often it
is haunted by ugly visions, and often broken by
violent leaps of the heart. Occasionally it is
disturbed also by noises never noticed at other
times. When the city lies all naked to the sun,
stripped by noon of every shadow, and empty of
wayfarers, the silence becomes amazing. In that
silence the papery rustle of a palm-leaf, or the
sudden sound of a lazy wavelet on the beach, —
like the clack of a thirsty tongue, — comes im-
mensely magnified to the ear. And this noon,
with its monstrous silence, is for the black people
the hour of ghosts. Everything alive is senseless
with the intoxication of light ; — even the woods
drowse and droop in their wrapping of lianas,
drunk with sun. . . .

Out of the siesta I used to be most often startled, not by sounds, but by something which I can
describe only as a sudden shock of thought.
This would follow upon a peculiar internal com-
motion caused, I believe, by some abnormal effect
of heat upon the lungs. A slow suffocating sensation would struggle up into the twilight-region between half-consciousness and real sleep, and there
bestir the ghastliest imaginings, — fancies and
fears of living burial. These would be accompanied by a voice, or rather the idea of a voice,
mocking and reproaching: — " ' *Truly the light
is sweet, and a pleasant thing it is for the eyes
to behold the sun.*' . . . Outside it is day, —
tropical day, — primeval day!   And you sleep!!
. . . ' *Though a man live many years and rejoice
in them all, yet* — ' . . . Sleep on! — all this
splendor will be the same when your eyes are
dust! . . . ' *Yet let him remember the days of
darkness;* — FOR THEY SHALL BE MANY!' "

How often, with that phantom crescendo in my
ears, have I leaped in terror from the hot couch,
to peer through the slatted shutters at the enormous light without — silencing, mesmerizing; —
then dashed cold water over my head, and stag-

gered back to the scorching mattress, again to
drowse, again to be awakened by the same voice,
or by the trickling of my own perspiration — a
feeling not always to be distinguished from that
caused by the running of a centipede! And how
I used to long for the night, with its Cross of the
South! Not because the night ever brought cool-
ness to the city, but because it brought relief from
the *weight* of that merciless sunfire. For the
feeling of such light is the feeling of a deluge of
something ponderable, — something that drowns
and dazzles and burns and numbs all at the same
time, and suggests the idea of liquified electricity.

There are times, however, when the tropical
heat seems only to thicken after sunset. On the
mountains the nights are, as a rule, delightful the
whole year round. They are even more delightful on the coast facing the trade-winds; and you
may sleep there in a seaward chamber, caressed
by a warm, strong breeze, — a breeze that plays
upon you not by gusts or whiffs, but with a
steady ceaseless blowing, — the great fanning
wind-current of the world's whirling. But in the
towns of the other coast — nearly all situated at
the base of wooded ranges cutting off the trade-

breeze, — the humid atmosphere occasionally becomes at night something nameless, — something worse than the air of an overheated conservatory. Sleep in such a medium is apt to be visited by nightmare of the most atrocious kind.

My personal experience was as follows: —

II

I was making a tour of the island with a half-breed guide; and we had to stop for one night in a small leeward-coast settlement, where we found accommodation at a sort of lodging-house kept by an aged widow. There were seven persons only in the house that night, — the old lady, her two daughters, two colored female-servants, myself and my guide. We were given a single-windowed room upstairs, rather small, — otherwise a typical, Creole bedroom, with bare clean floor, some heavy furniture of antique pattern, and a few rocking-chairs. There was in one corner a bracket supporting a sort of household shrine — what the Creoles call a *chapelle*. The shrine contained a white image of the Virgin before which a tiny light was floating in a cup of oil.

By colonial custom your servant, while travelling with you, sleeps either in the same room, or before the threshold; and my man simply lay down on a mat beside the huge four-pillared couch assigned to me, and almost immediately began to snore. Before getting into bed, I satisfied myself that the door was securely fastened.

The night stifled; — the air seemed to be coagulating. The single large window, overlooking a garden, had been left open, — but there was no movement in that atmosphere. Bats — very large bats, — flew soundlessly in and out; — one actually fanning my face with its wings as it circled over the bed. Heavy scents of ripe fruit — nauseously sweet — rose from the garden, where palms and plantains stood still as if made of metal. From the woods above the town stormed the usual night-chorus of tree-frogs, insects, and nocturnal birds, — a tumult not to be accurately described by any simile, but suggesting, through numberless sharp tinkling tones, the fancy of a wide slow cataract of broken glass. I tossed and turned on the hot hard bed, vainly trying to find one spot a little cooler than the rest. Then I rose, drew a rocking-chair to the window and lighted a cigar. The smoke hung motionless; after each puff, I had to blow it away. My man had ceased to snore. The bronze of his naked breast — shining with moisture under the faint light of the shrine-lamp, — showed no movement of respiration. He might have been a corpse. The heavy heat seemed always to become heavier. At last, utterly exhausted, I went back to bed, and slept.

It must have been well after midnight when I felt the first vague uneasiness, — *the suspicion*, — that precedes a nightmare. I was half-conscious, dream-conscious of the actual, — knew myself in that very room, — wanted to get up. Immediately the uneasiness grew into terror, because I found that I could not move. Something unutterable in the air was mastering will. I tried to cry out, and my utmost effort resulted only in a whisper too low for any one to hear. Simultaneously I became aware of a Step ascending the stair, — a muffled heaviness; and the real nightmare began, — the horror of the ghastly magnetism that held voice and limb, — the hopeless will-struggle against dumbness and impotence. The stealthy Step approached, — but with lentor malevolently measured, — slowly, slowly, as if

the stairs were miles deep. It gained the threshold, — waited. Gradually then, and without
sound, the locked door opened; and the Thing
entered, bending as it came, — a thing robed, —
feminine, — reaching to the roof, — not to be
looked at! A floor-plank creaked as It neared
the bed; — and then — with a frantic effort — I
woke, bathed in sweat; my heart beating as if it
were going to burst. The shrine-light had died:
in the blackness I could see nothing; but I thought
I heard that Step retreating. I certainly heard
the plank creak again. With the panic still upon
me, I was actually unable to stir. The wisdom
of striking a match occurred to me, but I dared
not yet rise. Presently, as I held my breath to
listen, a new wave of black fear passed through
me; for I heard moanings, — long nightmare
moanings, — moanings that seemed to be answering each other from two different rooms below.
And then, close to me, my guide began to moan,
— hoarsely, hideously. I cried to him: —

"Louis! — Louis!"

We both sat up at once. I heard him panting,
and I knew that he was fumbling for his cutlass
in the dark. Then, in a voice husky with fear, he
asked: —

" *Missiè, ess ou tanne ?* " [Monsieur, est-ce que vous entendez ?]

The moaners continued to moan, — always in crescendo: then there were sudden screams, — "*Madame !* " — " *Manzell !* " — and running of bare feet, and sounds of lamps being lighted, and, at last, a general clamor of frightened voices. I rose, and groped for the matches. The moans and the clamor ceased.

"*Missiè,*" my man asked again, "*ess ou tè ouè y ?* " [Monsieur, est-ce que vous l'avez vue ?]

— " *Ça ou le di ?* " [Qu'est-ce que vous voulez dire ?] I responded in bewilderment, as my fingers closed on the match-box.

— " *Fenm-là ?* " he answered. . . . THAT WOMAN ?

The question shocked me into absolute immobility. Then I wondered if I could have understood. But he went on in his patois, as if talking to himself : —

— " Tall, tall — high like this room, that Zombi. When She came the floor cracked. I heard — I saw."

After a moment, I succeeded in lighting a candle, and I went to the door. It was still locked, — double-locked. No human being could have entered through the high window.

—" Louis ! " I said, without believing what I said, — " you have been only dreaming."

—" Missié," he answered, " it was no dream. *She has been in all the rooms, touching people !* "

I said, —

—" That is foolishness ! See ! — the door is double-locked."

Louis did not even look at the door, but responded : —

—" Door locked, door not locked, Zombi comes and goes. . . . I do not like this house. . . . Missié, leave that candle burning ! "

He uttered the last phrase imperatively, without using the respectful *souplé* — just as a guide speaks at an instant of common danger ; and his tone conveyed to me the contagion of his fear. Despite the candle, I knew for one moment the sensation of nightmare outside of sleep ! The coincidences stunned reason ; and the hideous primitive fancy fitted itself, like a certitude, to the explanation of cause and effect. The similarity of my vision and the vision of Louis, the creaking of the floor heard by us both, the visit of the nightmare to every room in succession, — these formed a more than unpleasant combination of evidence. I tried the planking with my foot in

the place where I thought I had seen the figure:
it uttered the very same loud creak that I had
heard before. " *Ça pa ka sam rêvé,*" said Louis.
No! — that was not like dreaming. I left the
candle burning, and went back to bed — not to
sleep, but to think. Louis lay down again, with
his hand on the hilt of his cutlass.

I thought for a long time. All was now silent
below. The heat was at last lifting; and occa-
sional whiffs of cooler air from the garden announced the wakening of a land-breeze. Louis,
in spite of his recent terror, soon began to snore
again. Then I was startled by hearing a plank
creak — quite loudly, — the same plank that I had
tried with my foot. This time Louis did not
seem to hear it. There was nothing there. It
creaked twice more, — and I understood. The
intense heat first, and the change of temperature
later, had been successively warping and unwarp-
ing the wood so as to produce those sounds. In
the state of dreaming, which is the state of imperfect sleep, noises may be audible enough to
affect imagination strongly, — and may startle
into motion a long procession of distorted fancies.
At the same time it occurred to me that the al-

most concomitant experiences of nightmare in
the different rooms could be quite sufficiently explained by the sickening atmospheric oppression
of the hour.

There still remained the ugly similitude of
the two dreams to be accounted for; and a
natural solution of this riddle also, I was able to
find after some little reflection. The coincidence
had certainly been startling; but the similitude
was only partial. That which my guide had
seen in his nightmare was a familiar creation of
West-Indian superstition — probably of African
origin. But the shape that I had dreamed about
used to vex my sleep in childhood, — a phantom
created for me by the impression of a certain
horrible Celtic story which ought not to have
been told to any child blessed, or cursed, with an
imagination.

III

Musing on this experience led me afterwards
to think about the meaning of that fear which
we call "the fear of darkness," and yet is not
really fear of darkness. Darkness, as a simple

condition, never could have originated the feeling, — a feeling that must have preceded any definite idea of ghosts by thousands of ages. The inherited, instinctive fear, as exhibited by children, is not a fear of darkness in itself, but of indefinable danger associated with darkness. Evolutionally explained, this dim but voluminous terror would have for its primal element the impressions created by real experience — experience of something acting in darkness; — and the fear of the supernatural would mingle in it only as a much later emotional development. The primeval cavern-gloom lighted by nocturnal eyes; — the blackness of forest-gaps by river-marges, where destruction lay in wait to seize the thirsty; — the umbrages of tangled shores concealing horror; — the dusk of the python's lair; — the place of hasty refuge echoing the fury of famished brute and desperate man; — the place of burial, and the fancied frightful kinship of the buried to the cave-haunters : — all these, and countless other impressions of the relation of darkness to death, must have made that ancestral fear of the dark which haunts the imagination of the child, and still betimes seizes the adult as he sleeps in the security of civilization.

Not all the fear of dreams can be the fear of the immemorial. But that strange nightmare-sensation of being held by invisible power exerted from a distance — is it quite sufficiently explained by the simple suspension of will-power during sleep? Or could it be a composite inheritance of numberless memories of *having been caught*? Perhaps the true explanation would suggest no prenatal experience of monstrous mesmerisms nor of monstrous webs, — nothing more startling than the evolutional certainty that man, in the course of his development, has left behind him conditions of terror incomparably worse than any now existing. Yet enough of the psychological riddle of nightmare remains to tempt the question whether human organic memory holds no record of extinct forms of pain, — pain related to strange powers once exerted by some ghastly vanished life.

19

The Eternal Haunter

The Eternal Haunter

THIS year the Tōkyō color-prints — *Nishiki-é* — seem to me of unusual interest. They reproduce, or almost reproduce, the color-charm of the early broadsides; and they show a marked improvement in line-drawing. Certainly one could not wish for anything prettier than the best prints of the present season.

My latest purchase has been a set of weird studies, — spectres of all kinds known to the Far East, including many varieties not yet discovered in the West. Some are extremely unpleasant; but a few are really charming. Here, for example, is a delicious thing by "Chikanobu," just published, and for sale at the remarkable price of three *sen!*

Can you guess what it represents? . . . Yes, a girl, — but what kind of a girl? Study it a little. . . . Very lovely, is she not, with that shy sweetness in her downcast gaze, — that light and dainty grace, as of a resting butterfly? . . . No, she is not some Psyche of the most Eastern East, in the sense that you mean — but she is a soul. Observe that the cherry-flowers falling from the branch above, are passing *through* her form. See also the folds of her robe, below, melting into blue faint mist. How delicate and vapory the whole thing is! It gives you the feeling of spring; and all those fairy colors are the colors of a Japanese spring-morning. . . . No, she is not the personification of any season. Rather she is a dream — such a dream as might haunt the slumbers of Far-Eastern youth; but the artist did not intend her to represent a dream . . . You cannot guess? Well, she is a tree-spirit, — the Spirit of the Cherry-tree. Only in the twilight of morning or of evening she appears, gliding about her tree; — and whoever sees her must love her. But, if approached, she vanishes back into the trunk, like a vapor absorbed. There is a legend of one tree-spirit who loved a man, and even gave him a son; but such conduct was quite at variance with the shy habits of her race. . . .

You ask what is the use of drawing the Impossible? Your asking proves that you do not feel the charm of this vision of youth, — this dream of spring. *I* hold that the Impossible bears a

much closer relation to fact than does most of
what we call the real and the commonplace. The
Impossible may not be naked truth; but I think
that it is usually truth, — masked and veiled, perhaps, but eternal. Now to me this Japanese
dream is true, — true, at least, as human love is.
Considered even as a ghost it is true. Whoever
pretends not to believe in ghosts of any sort, lies
to his own heart. Every man is haunted by
ghosts. And this color-print reminds me of a
ghost whom we all know, — though most of us
(poets excepted) are unwilling to confess the
acquaintance.

Perhaps — for it happens to some of us — you
may have seen this haunter, in dreams of the
night, even during childhood. Then, of course,
you could not know the beautiful shape bending
above your rest: possibly you thought her to be
an angel, or the soul of a dead sister. But in
waking life we first become aware of her presence
about the time when boyhood begins to ripen
into youth.

This first of her apparitions is a shock of
ecstasy, a breathless delight; but the wonder and
the pleasure are quickly followed by a sense of

sadness inexpressible, — totally unlike any sadness ever felt before, — though in her gaze there is only caress, and on her lips the most exquisite of smiles. And you cannot imagine the reason of that feeling until you have learned who she is, — which is not an easy thing to learn.

Only a moment she remains; but during that luminous moment all the tides of your being set and surge to her with a longing for which there is not any word. And then — suddenly! — she is not; and you find that the sun has gloomed, the colors of the world turned grey.

Thereafter enchantment remains between you and all that you loved before, — persons or things or places. None of them will ever seem again so near and dear as in other days.

Often she will return. Once that you have seen her she will never cease to visit you. And this haunting, — ineffably sweet, inexplicably sad, — may fill you with rash desire to wander over the world in search of somebody like her. But however long and far you wander, never will you find that somebody.

Later you may learn to fear her visits because of the pain they bring, — the strange pain that you cannot understand. But the breadth of zones and seas cannot divide you from her; walls of iron cannot exclude her. Soundless and subtle as a shudder of ether is the motion of her.

Ancient her beauty as the heart of man, — yet ever waxing fairer, forever remaining young. Mortals wither in Time as leaves in the frost of autumn; but Time only brightens the glow and the bloom of her endless youth.

All men have loved her; — all must continue to love her. But none shall touch with his lips even the hem of her garment.

All men adore her; yet all she deceives, and many are the ways of her deception. Most often she lures her lover into the presence of some earthly maid, and blends herself incomprehensibly with the body of that maid, and works such sudden glamour that the human gaze becomes divine, — that the human limbs shine through their raiment. But presently the luminous haunter detaches herself from the mortal, and leaves her dupe to wonder at the mockery of sense.

No man can describe her, though nearly all men have some time tried to do so. Pictured she cannot be, — since her beauty itself is a ceaseless becoming, multiple to infinitude, and tremulous with perpetual quickening, as with flowing of light.

There is a story, indeed, that thousands of years ago some marvellous sculptor was able to fix in stone a single remembrance of her. But this doing became for many the cause of sorrow supreme ; and the Gods decreed, out of compassion, that to no other mortal should ever be given power to work the like wonder. In these years we can worship only ; — we cannot portray.

But who is she ? — what is she ? . . . Ah! that is what I wanted you to ask. Well, she has never had a name; but I shall call her a tree-spirit.

The Japanese say that you can exorcise a tree-spirit, — if you are cruel enough to do it, — simply by cutting down her tree.

But you cannot exorcise the Spirit of whom I speak, — nor ever cut down her tree.

For her tree is the measureless, timeless, billion-branching Tree of Life, — even the World-Tree, Yggdrasil, whose roots are in Night and Death, whose head is above the Gods.

Seek to woo her — she is Echo. Seek to clasp her — she is Shadow. But her smile will haunt you into the hour of dissolution and beyond, — through numberless lives to come.

And never will you return her smile, — never,

because of that which it awakens within you, — the pain that you cannot understand.

And never, never shall you win to her, — because she is the phantom light of long-expired suns, — because she was shaped by the beating of infinite millions of hearts that are dust, — because her witchery was made in the endless ebb and flow of the visions and hopes of youth, through countless forgotten cycles of your own incalculable past.